Reading
TUTOR 리딩튜터

Starter
2

Welcome to
Reading Tutor Starter

<리딩튜터 스타터> 시리즈는 **독해를 처음 시작하는 학생들을 위한 독해 전문서입니다.** 독해가 즐거워지는 놀라운 경험을 선사해 드리는 <리딩튜터 스타터> 시리즈가 3종으로 새롭게 탄생했어요. 다양한 분야의 소재를 재미있게 풀어낸 지문을 통해 영어 독해의 기초를 탄탄히 다져보세요. 즐거운 독해가 만드는 실력의 차이를 실감하게 될 거예요.

체계적인 학습을 위한 시리즈 구성 및 난이도

단어 수와 렉사일(Lexile) 지수를 기반으로 개발되어, 더욱 객관적으로 난이도를 비교·선택하실 수 있습니다.

70–90 words
200L–400L

90–110 words
300L–500L

100–120 words
400L–600L

독해의 기초를 다지는 <리딩튜터 스타터>만의 특징

- 독해를 처음 접하는 학생들이 흥미를 가질 수 있는 다채로운 소재를 선정하였습니다.
- 이해력을 높여주고 다양한 지식을 제공하는 Knowledge Bank 코너를 강화했습니다.
- 다양한 문제 유형을 통해 실질적인 독해 실력을 향상할 수 있습니다.

How to Study
Reading Tutor Starter

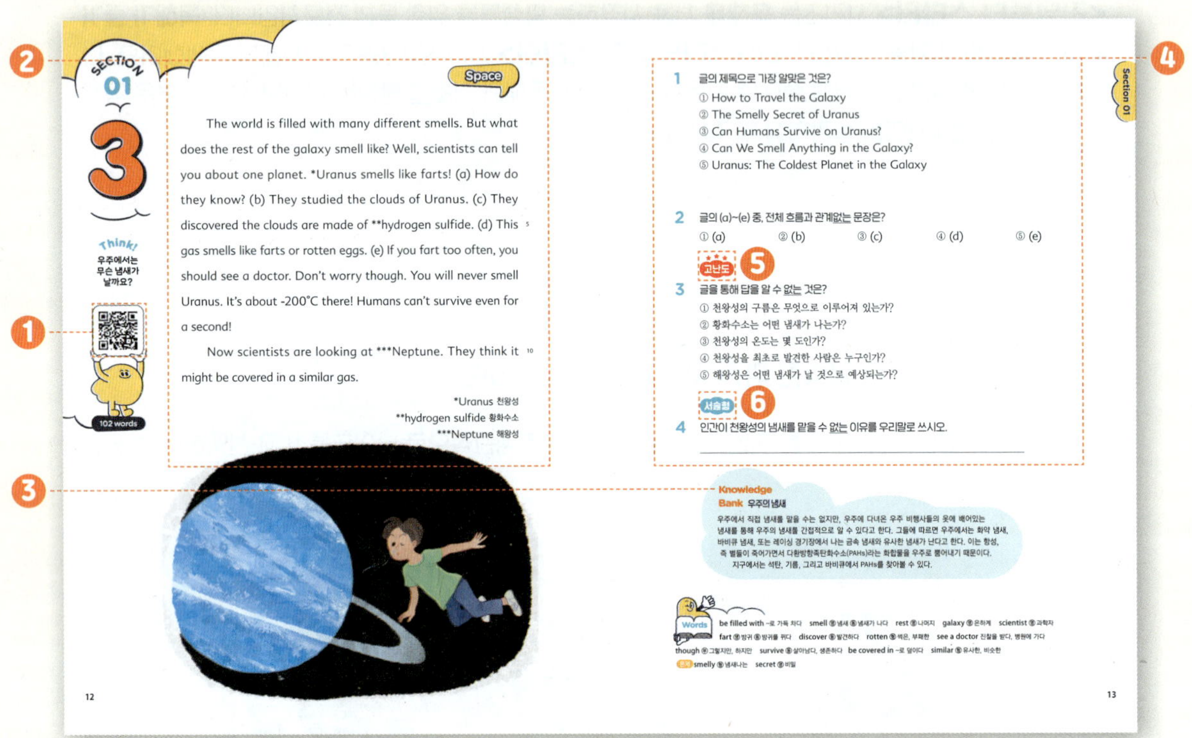

❶ QR코드

지문을 읽기 전에 녹음 파일을 듣고, 내용을 미리 파악해 보세요. 또, 학습 후 녹음 파일을 들으면서 복습할 수도 있어요.

❷ Reading

재미있고 상식도 쌓을 수 있는 지문을 읽어 보세요. 영어 독해 실력 향상은 물론, 상식을 넓히고 사고력도 기를 수 있어요.

❸ Knowledge Bank

지문 이해를 돕는 배경지식을 읽어 보세요. 지문이 이해가 안 될 때, 내용을 더 깊이 알고 싶을 때 큰 도움이 될 거예요.

❹ 최신 경향의 문제

최신 학습 경향을 반영한 다양한 문제를 풀어 보세요. 대의 파악부터 세부 정보 파악, 서술형 문제까지 정답을 보지 않고 스스로 푸는 것이 중요해요.

❺ 고난도

조금 어렵지만 풀고 나면 독해력이 한층 더 상승하는 것을 느낄 수 있어요. 한 번에 풀 수 없으면, 지문을 한 번 더 읽어 보세요.

❻ 서술형

서술형 문제로 독해력을 높이는 동시에 학교 내신 서술형 문제에도 대비할 수 있어요.

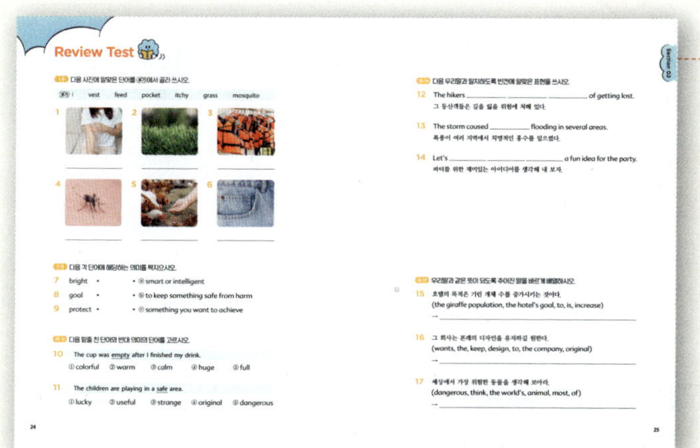

Review Test

각 섹션에서 배운 단어와 숙어를 반복 학습하고, 주요 문장과 구문을 복습해요. 단어와 숙어, 구문의 쓰임새를 더 잘 이해할 수 있어요.

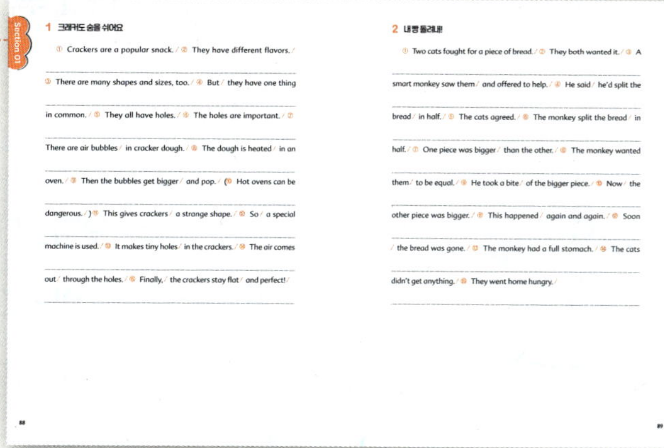

직독직해 워크시트

각 지문의 문장별 직독직해 훈련을 통해 배운 내용을 더 꼼꼼히 복습할 수 있어요.

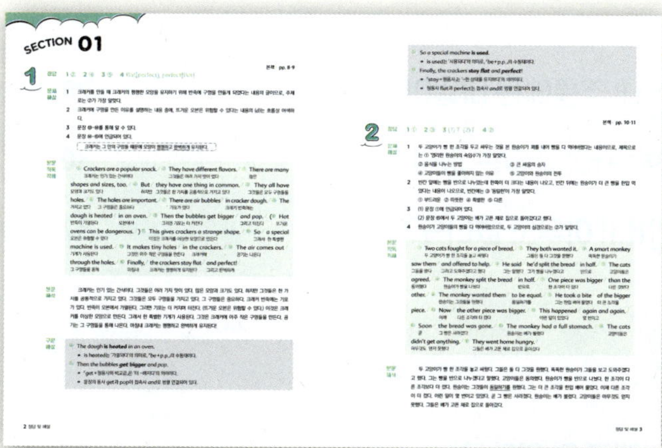

정답 및 해설

정답의 이유를 알려주는 문제 해설, 빠르게 해석할 수 있는 방법을 보여주는 직독직해, 한눈에 보는 본문 해석, 해석이 안 되는 부분이 없도록 도와주는 구문 해설로 알차게 구성했습니다.

어휘 암기장

본문에 나온 단어와 숙어를 한눈에 볼 수 있도록 정리했습니다. 간단한 확인 문제도 있으니, 가지고 다니며 암기하고 확인해 볼 수 있어요.

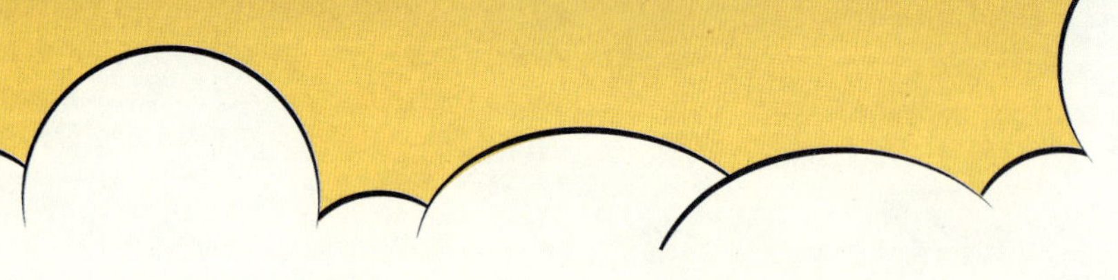

Contents

SECTION
01

1

Crackers are a popular snack. They have different flavors. There are many shapes and sizes, too. But they have one thing in common. They all have holes. The holes are important. (a) There are air bubbles in cracker dough. (b) The dough is heated in an oven. (c) Then the bubbles get bigger and pop. (d) Hot ovens can be dangerous. (e) This gives crackers a strange shape. So a special machine is used. It makes tiny holes in the crackers. The air comes out through the holes. Finally, the crackers stay flat and perfect!

1 글의 주제로 가장 알맞은 것은?

① 크래커를 발명한 사람

② 크래커에 구멍이 있는 이유

③ 최고의 크래커를 만드는 지역

④ 맛있는 크래커를 만드는 방법

⑤ 크래커에 공기 방울이 생기는 현상

2 글의 (a)~(e) 중, 전체 흐름과 관계<u>없는</u> 문장은?

① (a)　　　② (b)　　　③ (c)　　　④ (d)　　　⑤ (e)

3 글에 따르면, 밑줄 친 <u>a special machine</u>의 용도는?

① 크래커가 빨리 익게 하는 것

② 크래커의 반죽을 쉽게 만드는 것

③ 오븐에 화상을 입는 것을 막는 것

④ 크래커를 다양한 맛으로 만드는 것

⑤ 크래커에 공기가 나올 구멍을 만드는 것

서술형

4 다음 빈칸에 알맞은 단어를 글에서 찾아 쓰시오.

> Crackers remain __________ and __________ in shape because of the holes in them.

2

Two cats fought for a piece of bread. They both wanted it. A smart monkey saw them and offered to help. He said he'd split the bread in half. The cats agreed. The monkey split the bread in half. One piece was bigger than the other. The monkey wanted them to be ___________. He took a bite of the [5] bigger piece. Now the other piece was bigger. This happened again and again. Soon the bread was gone. The monkey had a full stomach. The cats didn't get anything. They went home hungry.

Think!
빵 하나를
절반으로
어떻게 나눌까요?

91 words

1 글의 제목으로 가장 알맞은 것은?

① A Clever Monkey's Trick
② How to Share Your Food
③ The Winner of a Big Fight
④ Why Cats Don't Like Bread
⑤ A Battle of Cats and Monkeys

2 글의 빈칸에 들어갈 말로 가장 알맞은 것은?

① soft　　② warm　　③ equal　　④ special　　⑤ different

3 글의 내용과 일치하면 T, 그렇지 않으면 F를 쓰시오.

(1) 두 고양이는 빵 한 조각을 가지고 싸우고 있었다. ____________

(2) 두 고양이는 배가 부른 채로 집으로 돌아갔다. ____________

4 두 고양이의 심경으로 가장 알맞은 것은?

① 행복한
② 화가 난
③ 신이 난
④ 감사해하는
⑤ 지루해하는

Words　fight ⑧ 싸우다(fight-fought-fought) ⑲ 싸움　a piece of 한 조각의　offer ⑧ 제공하다, (기꺼이) 해 주겠다고 하다　split ⑧ 분열되다; *나누다　in half 반으로　agree ⑧ 동의하다　take a bite of ~을 한입 먹다　happen ⑧ 일어나다　again and again 몇 번이고, 되풀이해서　have a full stomach 속이 든든하다, 배부르다　hungry ⑲ 배고픈　문제 clever ⑲ 영리한　trick ⑲ 속임수　share ⑧ 함께 쓰다; *나누다　winner ⑲ 승자　battle ⑲ 전투　soft ⑲ 부드러운　warm ⑲ 따뜻한　equal ⑲ (수·양·가치 등이) 동일한[같은]

3

Think!
우주에서는
무슨 냄새가
날까요?

102 words

The world is filled with many different smells. But what does the rest of the galaxy smell like? Well, scientists can tell you about one planet. *Uranus smells like farts! (a) How do they know? (b) They studied the clouds of Uranus. (c) They discovered the clouds are made of **hydrogen sulfide. (d) This gas smells like farts or rotten eggs. (e) If you fart too often, you should see a doctor. Don't worry though. You will never smell Uranus. It's about -200°C there! Humans can't survive even for a second!

Now scientists are looking at ***Neptune. They think it might be covered in a similar gas.

*Uranus 천왕성
**hydrogen sulfide 황화수소
***Neptune 해왕성

1 글의 제목으로 가장 알맞은 것은?

① How to Travel the Galaxy
② The Smelly Secret of Uranus
③ Can Humans Survive on Uranus?
④ Can We Smell Anything in the Galaxy?
⑤ Uranus: The Coldest Planet in the Galaxy

2 글의 (a)~(e) 중, 전체 흐름과 관계<u>없는</u> 문장은?

① (a)　　　② (b)　　　③ (c)　　　④ (d)　　　⑤ (e)

3 글을 통해 답을 알 수 <u>없는</u> 것은?

① 천왕성의 구름은 무엇으로 이루어져 있는가?
② 황화수소는 어떤 냄새가 나는가?
③ 천왕성의 온도는 몇 도인가?
④ 천왕성을 최초로 발견한 사람은 누구인가?
⑤ 해왕성은 어떤 냄새가 날 것으로 예상되는가?

4 인간이 천왕성의 냄새를 맡을 수 <u>없는</u> 이유를 우리말로 쓰시오.

Knowledge Bank 우주의 냄새

우주에서 직접 냄새를 맡을 수는 없지만, 우주에 다녀온 우주 비행사들의 옷에 배어있는
냄새를 통해 우주의 냄새를 간접적으로 알 수 있다고 한다. 그들에 따르면 우주에서는 화약 냄새,
바비큐 냄새, 또는 레이싱 경기장에서 나는 금속 냄새와 유사한 냄새가 난다고 한다. 이는 항성,
즉 별들이 죽어가면서 다환방향족탄화수소(PAHs)라는 화합물을 우주로 뿜어내기 때문이다.
지구에서는 석탄, 기름, 그리고 바비큐에서 PAHs를 찾아볼 수 있다.

Words be filled with ~로 가득 차다　smell 몡 냄새 동 냄새가 나다　rest 몡 나머지　galaxy 몡 은하계　scientist 몡 과학자
fart 몡 방귀 동 방귀를 뀌다　discover 동 발견하다　rotten 혱 썩은, 부패한　see a doctor 진찰을 받다, 병원에 가다
though 뷔 그렇지만, 하지만　survive 동 살아남다, 생존하다　be covered in ~로 덮이다　similar 혱 유사한, 비슷한
문제 smelly 혱 냄새나는　secret 몡 비밀

13

Review Test

1-6 다음 사진에 알맞은 단어를 보기에서 골라 쓰시오.

보기 | bubble　　fight　　dough　　scientist　　smell　　split

1	2	3

____

4	5	6

____

7-9 다음 각 단어에 해당하는 의미를 짝지으시오.

7　trick　　•　　　　•　ⓐ to make something warm or hot

8　heat　　•　　　　•　ⓑ to find out something unknown

9　discover　•　　　　•　ⓒ a clever way to fool someone

10-11 다음 밑줄 친 단어와 반대 의미의 단어를 고르시오.

10　The cookie was <u>soft</u> and sweet.

　　① flat　　② warm　　③ hard　　④ popular　　⑤ important

11　These two shirts look very <u>similar</u> in color.

　　① equal　　② strange　　③ tiny　　④ rotten　　⑤ different

12-14 다음 우리말과 일치하도록 빈칸에 알맞은 표현을 쓰시오.

12 He wanted to ______________ ______________ ______________ ______________
the delicious, hot pizza.

그는 그 맛있고 뜨거운 피자를 한입 먹고 싶었다.

13 You should ______________ ______________ ______________ if the pain doesn't
go away.

통증이 없어지지 않으면 너는 병원에 가야 한다.

14 What do you and your sister ______________ ______________ ______________?

너와 너의 언니는 무엇을 공통적으로 가지고 있니?

15-17 우리말과 같은 뜻이 되도록 주어진 말을 바르게 배열하시오.

15 그러면 기포는 더 커지며 터진다.

(pop, the bubbles, bigger, get, and)

→ Then ____.

16 세상은 다양한 냄새로 가득 차 있다.

(filled, the world, smells, with, is, many different)

→ ____

17 한 조각이 다른 것보다 더 컸다.

(the other, bigger, one piece, than, was)

→ ____

방콕의 신비로운 새벽 사원

다음 실선을 따라 한 선으로 왓 아룬을 그려보세요.

태국의 10바트 동전에 그려져 있는 왓 아룬은 방콕에 위치한 100년 이상의 전통을 자랑하는 사원이에요. 이곳은 중앙의 높은 탑과 주변의 작은 4개의 탑으로 구성되어 있어요. 탑들의 높이는 66.8m에서 86m에 이르는데요. 중앙의 거대한 탑은 힌두교의 시바신을 상징한다고 해요. '아룬'은 태국어로 새벽을 의미해서 왓 아룬을 '새벽 사원'이라고도 부르는데, 이른 아침 햇빛에 반사되는 탑들의 모습이 찬란하여 이런 이름이 붙여졌다고 합니다. 민소매, 짧은 바지나 치마를 입으면 입장에 제한을 받을 수 있으니 주의하세요!

SECTION
02

1

95 words

Think of the world's most dangerous animal. Are they snakes? Sharks? Bears? The answer may surprise you. It is mosquitoes.

Why are mosquitoes so dangerous? You might not worry about an itchy mosquito bite. But it can become a big problem. 5 Many mosquitoes carry diseases. These diseases can spread when they bite humans. Such diseases can be deadly.

So, how can you protect yourself from mosquitoes? Avoiding mosquito bites is the best way. Wear a long-sleeved shirt outside. Wear long pants, too. Then mosquitoes cannot 10 bite you easily. It may be hotter, but it is ______________!

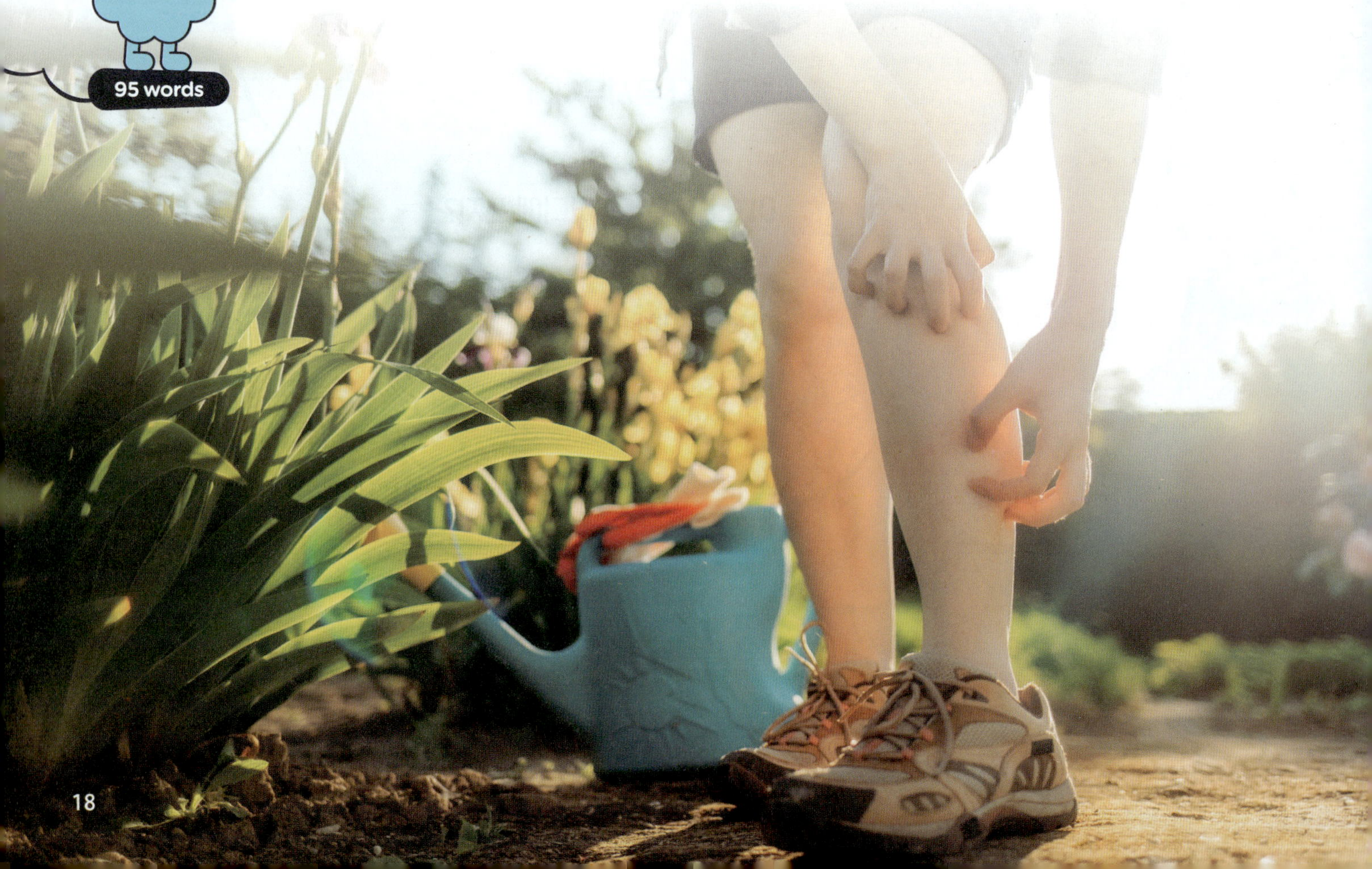

1 글의 주제로 가장 알맞은 것은?

① 질병 예방의 중요성
② 야생동물을 보호하는 이유
③ 더운 날씨에 적절한 옷차림
④ 세계에서 가장 위험한 동물
⑤ 모기에 물렸을 때 대처하는 법

2 글의 내용과 일치하면 T, 그렇지 않으면 F를 쓰시오.

(1) 모기가 옮기는 질병들은 사람의 생명에 치명적일 수 있다. ____________

(2) 모기는 소매가 긴 옷에 잘 달라붙는다. ____________

고난도

3 글의 빈칸에 들어갈 말로 가장 알맞은 것은?

① safer　　　　② longer　　　　③ calmer
④ less helpful　　⑤ more harmful

서술형

4 다음 빈칸에 알맞은 단어를 글에서 찾아 쓰시오.

> Mosquitoes are the most ___________ because they can carry deadly
> ___________.

2

Have you seen strange, tiny pockets on your jeans? You cannot put much in them. So, what are they for? Well, back in the late 1800s, people had *pocket watches! Workers usually put their watches in their vests. But their watches often fell out and broke. 5

Denim jeans company founder Levi Strauss came up with a bright idea: a watch pocket! Workers could finally keep their watches in a safe place. Today few people carry pocket watches. However, the company wants to keep the original design. So the pockets have stayed. The next time you see that little pocket, remember it was once ______________! 15

*pocket watch 회중시계(휴대용 소형 시계)

Knowledge Bank 리바이 스트라우스
(Levi Strauss, 1829~1902)

리바이 스트라우스는 독일계 유대인으로, 세계 최초로 청바지 생산 공장을 설립했다. 그는 광부들이 해진 바지를 꿰매 입는 모습을 보고, 군용 천막으로 쓰이던 질긴 천으로 바지를 만들기 시작했다. 그가 만든 바지가 점점 인기를 얻자, 후에 훨씬 더 질긴 데님 천으로 바지를 만들고 푸른색으로 염색하여 튼튼한 청바지를 시장에 선보였다.

1 글의 제목으로 가장 알맞은 것은?

① Choosing the Best Pocket Watch
② The Origin of Tiny Pockets on Jeans
③ What Did Workers Wear in the 1800s?
④ Who Made the First Jeans with Pockets?
⑤ The First Denim Jeans Company in the World

2 글의 빈칸에 들어갈 말로 가장 알맞은 것은?

① huge   ② empty   ③ unique   ④ useful   ⑤ colorful

3 다음 빈칸에 알맞은 표현을 글에서 찾아 쓰시오.

> The tiny pockets on jeans were designed for workers' __________ __________.

4 오늘날 청바지에 작은 주머니가 그대로 있는 이유를 우리말로 쓰시오.

____

Words pocket 몡 주머니   vest 몡 조끼   fall out 떨어져 나가다   break 동 깨어지다, 부서지다; *고장 나다(break-broke-broken)
founder 몡 창립자, 설립자   come up with ~을 생각해 내다, (해답 등을) 찾아내다   bright 형 밝은; *똑똑한, 영리한
place 몡 장소   carry 동 나르다; *가지고 다니다   original 형 원래의, 본래의   stay 동 계속 있다, 그대로 남다   remember 동 기억하다
once 뮈 한 번; *(과거) 한때   문제 origin 몡 기원, 유래   huge 형 거대한   empty 형 비어 있는, 빈   useful 형 유용한
colorful 형 형형색색의

3

Think!
멸종 위기의
동물을 돕는 단체를
알고 있나요?

113 words

Do you love animals? Then this hotel in Nairobi, Kenya is for you. It is next to a protected area with a group of Rothschild's giraffes. These giraffes are at risk in the wild. (a) The hotel was first built in 1932. (b) And it started to protect giraffes in the 1970s. (c) The hotel's goal is to increase the giraffe population. (d) Healthy giraffes can live for 25 years in the wild. (e) The hotel is slowly returning the giraffes to the wild. Hotel guests can see the giraffes up close. If they are lucky, they can also feed them. Giraffes love to eat grass *pellets at breakfast. Where else can you enjoy breakfast with a giraffe?

*pellet (부드러운 것을 단단하게 뭉친) 알갱이

1 글의 제목으로 가장 알맞은 것은?

① What Do Giraffes Eat?
② A Hotel for Tourists and Giraffes
③ Nairobi: The Best Place for Animals
④ Why Are Rothschild's Giraffes in Danger?
⑤ Animal-Friendly Hotels around the World

2 호텔에 관한 글의 내용과 일치하지 <u>않는</u> 것은?

① 케냐 나이로비에 위치해 있다.
② 1930년대에 건설되었다.
③ 기린을 보호하는 역할을 한다.
④ 투숙객은 기린을 가까이에서 볼 수 있다.
⑤ 투숙객이 기린에게 먹이를 주는 행위는 금지이다.

3 글의 (a)~(e) 중, 전체 흐름과 관계<u>없는</u> 문장은?

① (a)　　② (b)　　③ (c)　　④ (d)　　⑤ (e)

4 다음 질문에 우리말로 답하시오.

> Q: What is the goal of the hotel?

Words　protected area 보호 구역　be at risk 위험에 처하다　wild 몡 야생 (상태)　goal 몡 골; *목표　increase 몸 증가시키다, 늘리다　population 몡 인구; *개체 수　healthy 혱 건강한　return 몸 돌아오다; *돌려보내다　guest 몡 손님; *투숙객　up close 바로 가까이에서　lucky 혱 운이 좋은　feed 몸 먹이를 주다　grass 몡 풀　breakfast 몡 아침(밥), 아침 식사
문제　tourist 몡 관광객　danger 몡 위험

Review Test

1-6 다음 사진에 알맞은 단어를 보기 에서 골라 쓰시오.

| 보기 | vest | feed | pocket | itchy | grass | mosquito |

1 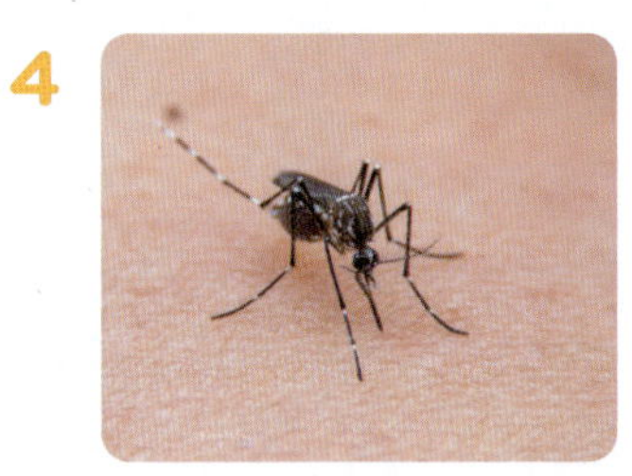

2 

3 

4

5

6

7-9 다음 각 단어에 해당하는 의미를 짝지으시오.

7 bright •   • ⓐ smart or intelligent

8 goal •   • ⓑ to keep something safe from harm

9 protect •   • ⓒ something you want to achieve

10-11 다음 밑줄 친 단어와 반대 의미의 단어를 고르시오.

10 The cup was <u>empty</u> after I finished my drink.

① colorful   ② warm   ③ calm   ④ huge   ⑤ full

11 The children are playing in a <u>safe</u> area.

① lucky   ② useful   ③ strange   ④ original   ⑤ dangerous

12-14 다음 우리말과 일치하도록 빈칸에 알맞은 표현을 쓰시오.

12 The hikers ___________ ___________ ___________ of getting lost.
그 등산객들은 길을 잃을 위험에 처해 있다.

13 The storm caused ___________ flooding in several areas.
폭풍이 여러 지역에서 치명적인 홍수를 일으켰다.

14 Let's ___________ ___________ ___________ a fun idea for the party.
파티를 위한 재미있는 아이디어를 생각해 내 보자.

15-17 우리말과 같은 뜻이 되도록 주어진 말을 바르게 배열하시오.

15 호텔의 목적은 기린 개체 수를 증가시키는 것이다.
(the giraffe population, the hotel's goal, to, is, increase)
→ ____

16 그 회사는 본래의 디자인을 유지하길 원한다.
(wants, the, keep, design, to, the company, original)
→ ____

17 세상에서 가장 위험한 동물을 생각해 보아라.
(dangerous, think, the world's, animal, most, of)
→ ____

크리스마스에는
독일의 크리스마스 마켓으로!

다음 그림에 숨겨진 물건들을 찾아보세요.

숨은 그림 그릇, 토끼, 칫솔, 당근, 가위

독일의 크리스마스 마켓은 600년 이상의 오랜 역사를 지녔다고 합니다. 보통 11월 말부터 시작해서 크리스마스이브인 12월 24일까지 독일 전역에서 130개 이상의 크리스마스 마켓이 열리는데요. 마켓마다 각 도시의 독특한 분위기가 녹아 있고 그곳의 공연, 음식, 수공예품을 구경하고 즐기다 보면 마치 동화 속에 들어와 있는 것 같은 기분을 느낄 수 있다고 해요. 꼭 한번 가보고 싶지 않나요?

SECTION
03

1 Animals
내 주름에는 비밀이 있어!

2 Food
하룻밤 사이에 무슨 일이?!

3 Culture
거기 아무도 없나요?

SECTION 03

1

Think!

코끼리는 어떠한 신체 특징을 가지고 있나요?

111 words

There are many ways to stay cool in the animal world. Kangaroos lick their arms. Dogs stick out their tongues. But elephants can't do either. They have other special ways to keep cool. One is their wrinkly skin! The wrinkles don't mean they are old! (a) Even young elephants have them. (b) Elephants can ⁵ drink 200 liters of water at one time. (c) The wrinkles keep five to ten times more water than smooth skin. (d) That means it takes longer for their skin to dry out. (e) This is great for staying cool longer in hot and dry Africa. Elephants in Asia live in wetter forests, so they have fewer wrinkles than ones in Africa. ¹⁰

Knowledge Bank 코끼리의 체온 조절법

인간은 땀이 증발하면서 체온이 내려가는데, 인간과 달리 코끼리는 땀샘이 없다. 코끼리 피부에 있는 수분이 땀과 같은 역할을 한다. 많은 주름은 더 많은 수분을 보유할 수 있게 도와주는 것이다. 또한, 코끼리는 체온을 조절하기 위해 커다란 귀를 사용하기도 한다. 코끼리의 귀에는 무수히 많은 혈관이 있는데, 귀를 펄럭거리면서 혈관 속 혈액의 온도를 낮출 수 있다.

1 글의 제목으로 가장 알맞은 것은?

① Different Types of Elephants
② Interesting Animals in Africa
③ Various Purposes of Wrinkles
④ Efforts to Protect Wild Elephants
⑤ How Elephants Keep Their Bodies Cool

2 글의 (a)~(e) 중, 전체 흐름과 관계<u>없는</u> 문장은?

① (a)　　　② (b)　　　③ (c)　　　④ (d)　　　⑤ (e)

3 코끼리에 관한 글의 내용과 일치하면 T, 그렇지 않으면 F를 쓰시오.

(1) 몸을 시원하게 하기 위해서 캥거루와 같은 방법을 사용한다. ＿＿＿＿＿

(2) 나이가 많을수록 몸에 주름이 많다. ＿＿＿＿＿

서술형

4 아시아의 코끼리가 아프리카의 코끼리보다 주름이 적은 이유를 우리말로 쓰시오.

＿＿＿＿＿＿＿＿＿＿＿＿＿＿＿＿＿＿＿＿＿＿＿＿＿＿＿＿＿＿＿＿＿

Words stay ⑧ 머무르다; *(상태를) 유지하다, ~인 채로 있다　cool ⑲ 시원한, 서늘한　lick ⑧ 핥다　stick out ~을 내밀다
tongue ⑲ 혀　wrinkly ⑲ 주름이 있는(wrinkle ⑲ 주름)　liter ⑲ 리터(부피의 단위)　smooth ⑲ 매끈한, 매끄러운
wet ⑲ 젖은, 습한　forest ⑲ 숲　**문제** type ⑲ 유형, 종류　various ⑲ 여러 가지의, 다양한　purpose ⑲ 목적　effort ⑲ 노력

2

A *popsicle is a frozen treat on a stick. Many American kids enjoy it in summer. Do you know this treat's interesting story? Actually, it came from a kid's ______________.

It was winter in 1905. Frank Epperson was 11 years old. He was making up a drink. He mixed sweet soda powder and water with a stick. He left his drink on the porch with the stick still in it. He completely forgot about it. He came back the next day. The drink was frozen! But he didn't throw it away. Instead, he licked it. Wow! It was delicious. The first popsicle was born.

*popsicle (막대기가 있는) 아이스캔디

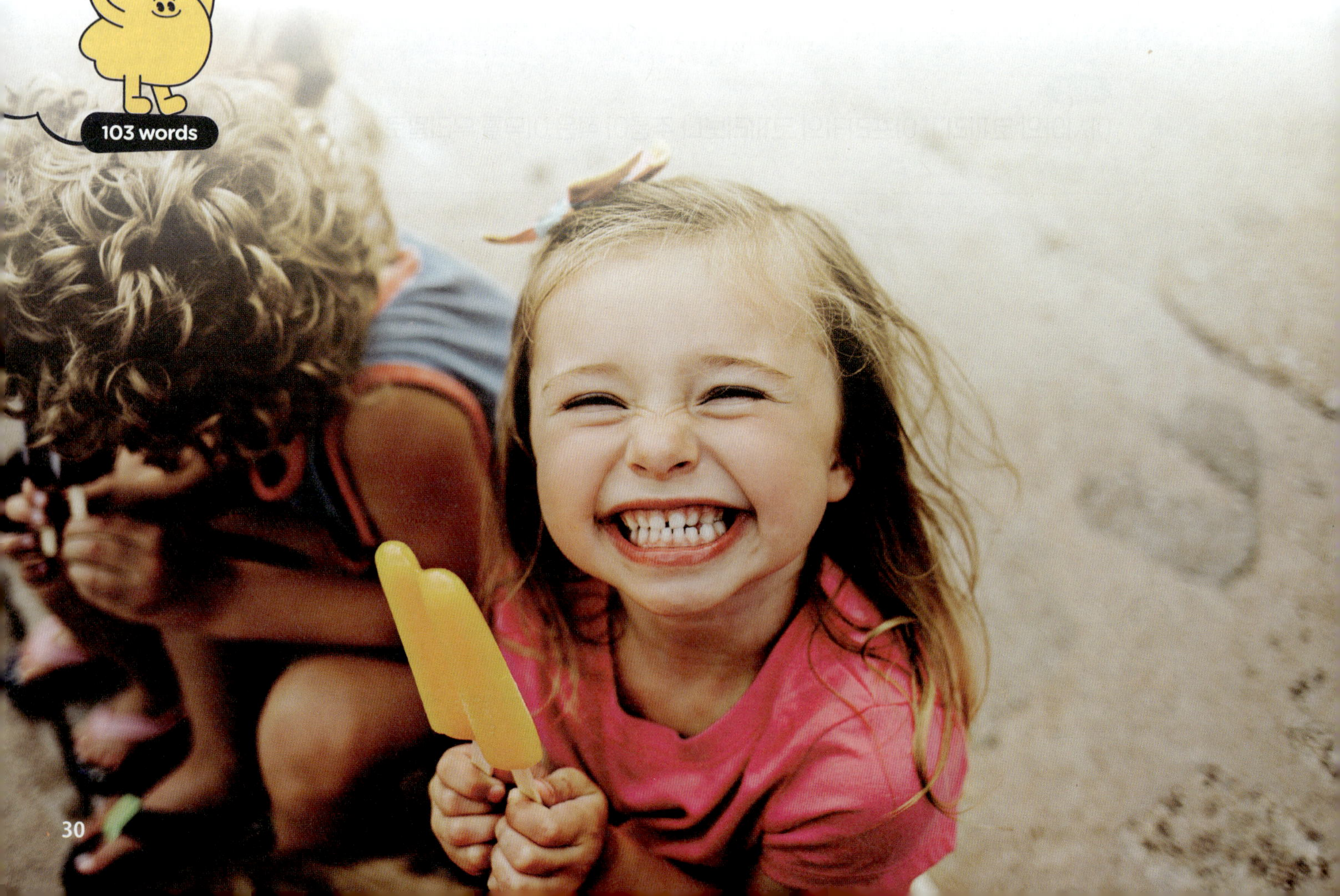

1 글의 주제로 가장 알맞은 것은?

① American kids' favorite snack
② the invention of the first popsicle
③ how to make your own popsicles
④ the most popular popsicle flavors
⑤ Frank Epperson's popsicle business

고난도

2 글의 빈칸에 들어갈 말로 가장 알맞은 것은?

① effort　　② mistake　　③ parents　　④ homework　　⑤ business

3 글의 내용과 일치하면 T, 그렇지 않으면 F를 쓰시오.

(1) 최초의 아이스캔디를 만들 때 물이 사용되었다.　　————————

(2) 최초의 아이스캔디는 냉동실에 보관된 후 만들어졌다.　　————————

서술형

4 다음 빈칸에 알맞은 단어를 보기에서 골라 쓰시오.

보기 | 　drink　　stick　　popsicle　　story

Frank Epperson made the first ____________ when he left a mixed ____________ on his porch overnight.

Words frozen ⑬냉동된　treat ⑲특별한 것[선물]; *간식　stick ⑲막대기　interesting ⑬흥미로운　come from ~에서 나오다, 비롯되다　make up ~을 만들다　drink ⑲음료　mix ⑧섞다(mixed ⑬혼합된)　sweet ⑬달콤한　soda ⑲탄산음료　powder ⑲가루　porch ⑲(건물 입구에 지붕이 얹혀 있고 흔히 벽이 둘러진) 현관　still ⑨아직, 여전히　completely ⑨완전히　forget ⑧잊다(forget-forgot-forgotten)　throw away 버리다　instead ⑨대신에　be born 태어나다　**문제** invention ⑲발명　flavor ⑲맛　mistake ⑲실수　business ⑲사업　overnight ⑨밤사이에, 하룻밤 동안

3

116 words

Most people around the world have lively New Year's parties. But the Balinese welcome their New Year differently. They celebrate it with Nyepi!

Nyepi is a day of ____________. It takes place on the first day of the Balinese *saka* calendar. It starts at 6 a.m. and continues for 24 hours. On this day, people clear their minds. They don't make any noise. This helps keep the balance between nature and humans. No planes fly and no restaurants open. People should stay indoors on Nyepi. The Balinese think demons will be fooled if all is quiet on Nyepi. The demons will think no one is there and leave. This will bring good luck and peace to Bali.

*saka 사카(태음력을 바탕으로 하는 힌두 고유의 달력)

Knowledge Bank 오고오고(Ogoh Ogoh)

녜삐 전날에는 전야제가 열린다. 이날 사람들은 대나무, 종이로 만든 '오고오고'라는 인형을 메고 징을 치며 마을을 행진하는데, 이 인형은 악령을 상징한다. 각 가정에서는 악령을 내쫓기 위해 냄비를 치는 등 큰 소리를 내며 집안을 돈다. 보통 마을 입구에서 시작되는 행렬은 인근 바닷가에 이르면 끝이 나는데, 이때 전통 의식과 함께 오고오고를 태워서 재를 날린다. 이는 인간으로부터 악령과 재앙을 멀리 쫓아내는 의미가 있다.

1 글의 주제로 가장 알맞은 것은?

① 새해 기념 행사들
② 자연과 인간의 균형
③ 다양한 국가들의 새해 풍습
④ 새해에 발리에서 갈만한 장소들
⑤ 발리 사람들이 새해를 맞이하는 방법

2 글의 빈칸에 들어갈 말로 가장 알맞은 것은?

① fun　　② noise　　③ horror　　④ sadness　　⑤ silence

3 Nyepi에 관한 글의 내용과 일치하지 <u>않는</u> 것은?

① 발리의 새해를 기념하는 날이다.
② 발리식 사카 달력의 첫날이다.
③ 오전 6시에 시작해서 저녁 6시에 끝난다.
④ 자연과 인간 사이의 균형을 유지하는 날이다.
⑤ 비행기가 날지 않는다.

4 다음 질문에 대한 답으로 가장 알맞은 것은?

> Q: Why do people stay inside quietly on Nyepi?

① 집 안을 깨끗이 청소하려고
② 악령들을 속여 떠나게 하려고
③ 가족들과 조용히 시간을 보내려고
④ 바깥에 돌아다니는 악령들을 피하려고
⑤ 전날 시끄러운 파티를 하여 휴식하려고

Words
lively ⑱ 활기 넘치는　Balinese ⑲ 발리 사람 ⑱ 발리의　welcome ⑧ 맞이하다, 환영하다　celebrate ⑧ 기념하다, 축하하다　take place 개최되다, 일어나다　calendar ⑲ 달력　continue ⑧ 계속되다[하다]　clear ⑧ 깨끗하게 하다　make noise 소리[소음]를 내다　balance ⑲ 균형　nature ⑲ 자연　plane ⑲ 비행기　indoors ⑨ 실내에서　demon ⑲ 악령, 귀신　fool ⑧ 속이다　quiet ⑱ 조용한　leave ⑧ 떠나다　bring ⑧ 가져다주다　peace ⑲ 평화　[문제] horror ⑲ 공포　sadness ⑲ 슬픔　silence ⑲ 고요, 침묵　quietly ⑨ 조용히

Review Test

1-6 다음 사진에 알맞은 단어를 보기에서 골라 쓰시오.

보기 | wrinkle　　nature　　frozen　　lick　　powder　　calendar

1 

2 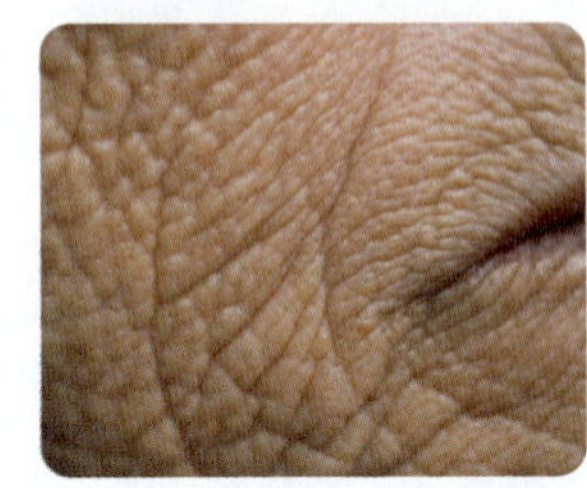

3 

4 

5 

6 

7-9 다음 각 단어에 해당하는 의미를 짝지으시오.

7　mistake　•　　　• ⓐ full of interest or energy

8　lively　•　　　• ⓑ a large area with many trees

9　forest　•　　　• ⓒ something you do wrong by accident

10-11 다음 밑줄 친 단어와 반대 의미의 단어를 고르시오.

10　The rain made the ground <u>wet</u>.

　① sweet　② dry　③ cool　④ smooth　⑤ interesting

11　Don't <u>forget</u> to turn off the lights.

　① leave　② stay　③ continue　④ bring　⑤ remember

12-14 다음 우리말과 일치하도록 빈칸에 알맞은 표현을 쓰시오.

12 The concert will _____________ _____________ next Saturday.

그 콘서트는 다음 주 토요일에 개최될 것이다.

13 He _____________ _____________ in a small town.

그는 작은 마을에서 태어났다.

14 Passengers in the aisle seats should not _____________ _____________ their legs.

통로 좌석의 승객들은 다리를 내밀지 말아야 한다.

15-17 우리말과 같은 뜻이 되도록 주어진 말을 바르게 배열하시오.

15 그는 음료수를 만들고 있었다.

(a drink, making up, he, was)

→ ____

16 이는 자연과 인간 사이의 균형을 유지하는 것을 돕는다.

(this, between, the balance, nature, helps, humans, and, keep)

→ ____

17 그것은 그들의 피부가 건조해지는 데 더 오래 걸린다는 것을 의미한다.

(dry out, for their skin, takes, it, longer, to)

→ That means _____________________________________.

페루의 공중도시 마추픽추

수수께끼를 간직한 도시 마추픽추를 자유롭게 색칠해 보세요.

페루 안데스산맥 해발 2,400m에 위치한 고대 잉카제국의 도시 마추픽추는 아직까지 베일에 싸여 있는 유적지입니다. 1911년에 마추픽추가 발견되기까지 아무도 그 존재를 몰랐다고 하는데요. 절벽과 밀림에 가려 아래에서는 볼 수 없고 공중에 올라서야 제대로 볼 수 있기 때문에 '공중도시'라고도 불린답니다. 마추픽추는 1983년 유네스코 세계문화유산에 등재되었으며, 누가 왜 이 도시를 만들었는지 아직까지도 정확히 밝혀지지 않았다고 해요.

SECTION
04

SECTION 04

1

111 words

Let's play a fun game. It's called Down, Down, Down. First, find a partner. Stand about 10 steps away from each other. (A) However, if you drop the ball, you must go down on one knee. (B) If no one drops the ball for a long time, each player takes a step back. (C) Then gently throw a tennis ball back and forth. 5 Then the game continues. On the second drop, you must kneel on both knees. After that, you have to place one elbow on the floor and then put down the other. The final body part to go down is the chin. If you drop the ball again, you lose the game.

1 글의 주제로 가장 알맞은 것은?

① the origins of a popular sport
② the rules of an interesting game
③ an easy way to exercise together
④ where a game's name comes from
⑤ how to win games without cheating

2 문장 (A)~(C)를 글의 흐름에 알맞게 배열한 것은?

① (A)-(B)-(C) 　② (A)-(C)-(B) 　③ (B)-(A)-(C)
④ (C)-(A)-(B) 　⑤ (C)-(B)-(A)

3 다음 질문에 우리말로 답하시오.

> Q: What should you do if you drop the ball two times?

____

4 다음 빈칸에 알맞은 단어를 글에서 찾아 쓰시오.

> The last body part to touch the ground is your __________. If you drop the
> ball after that, you __________ the game.

step ⑲ 걸음　away ⑨ 떨어져　drop ⑧ 떨어뜨리다 ⑲ 낙하　knee ⑲ 무릎(kneel ⑧ 무릎 꿇다)　player ⑲ 참가자[선수]
gently ⑨ 부드럽게　throw ⑧ 던지다　back and forth 왔다 갔다　continue ⑧ 계속되다　place ⑧ 놓다[두다]
elbow ⑲ 팔꿈치　chin ⑲ 턱　lose ⑧ 잃어버리다; *(경기에서) 지다　**문제** origin ⑲ 기원, 유래　rule ⑲ 규칙　exercise ⑧ 운동하다
cheating ⑲ 부정행위　ground ⑲ 땅바닥, 지면

2

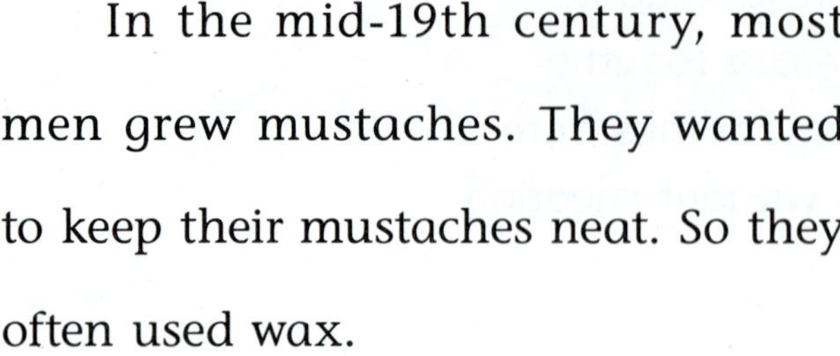

In the mid-19th century, most men grew mustaches. They wanted to keep their mustaches neat. So they often used wax.

However, this made enjoying tea difficult. Hot tea could melt the wax or get their mustaches wet. It was a big problem for them. Harvey Adams, a British potter, had an idea. In England during the 1860s, he invented the mustache cup! This special cup had a small barrier. It protected the mustache by covering it. It also had a small hole to drink through.

Finally a gentleman could have a handsome mustache and enjoy his tea time. Soon mustache cups became popular all over Europe.

Think!
사진에 있는 컵은 어떤 용도일까요?

106 words

1 글의 주제로 가장 알맞은 것은?

① tea culture in England
② why wax is not good for your skin
③ fashion styles of English gentlemen
④ the invention of cups for mustaches
⑤ why men grew mustaches in the 1800s

2 다음 질문에 우리말로 답하시오.

> Q: What problem did men with mustaches have when they enjoyed hot tea?

____

3 글에 따르면, 밑줄 친 <u>a small barrier</u>의 용도는?

① 차가 빨리 식는 것을 막음
② 차가 엎질러지는 것을 막음
③ 차를 급히 마시는 것을 막음
④ 차에 화상을 입는 것을 막음
⑤ 차가 콧수염을 망가뜨리는 것을 막음

4 mustache cup에 관한 글의 내용과 일치하면 T, 그렇지 않으면 F를 쓰시오.

(1) 영국의 도예가에 의해 발명되었다. ____________

(2) 유럽에서 크게 인기를 끌지 못했다. ____________

Words   **grow** ⑧ 커지다; *기르다(grow-grew-grown)   **mustache** ⑲ 콧수염   **neat** ⑱ 정돈된, 단정한, 깔끔한   **melt** ⑧ 녹이다[녹다]
potter ⑲ 도예가   **invent** ⑧ 발명하다   **barrier** ⑲ 장벽, 벽   **cover** ⑧ (보호하기 위해) 가리다, 씌우다   **hole** ⑲ 구덩이, 구멍
gentleman ⑲ 신사, 양반   문제   **culture** ⑲ 문화   **invention** ⑲ 발명

3

113 words

▲ 주세페 아르침볼도의 〈베르툼누스〉

You might think *Renaissance art is very boring. But Giuseppe Arcimboldo's work is fun. He was an artist of the 16th century. He painted some playful portraits. From a distance, they look like people. But look closely! (a) Those people are made of various items such as food, flowers, and books.

(b) An example of his work is *The Vegetable Gardener*. (c) It is a painting of vegetables in a bowl. (d) You can get healthy vitamins from vegetables. (e) When you turn the painting upside down, someone is smiling at you! The onion is

▲ 주세페 아르침볼도의 〈채소 기르는 사람〉

a fat cheek, the large **parsnip is a long nose, and the mushrooms are lips. Which items would you use for your portrait?

*Renaissance 르네상스(14~16세기 유럽의 문화 운동)
**parsnip 파스닙(당근과 비슷하게 생긴 채소)

1 글의 제목으로 가장 알맞은 것은?

① How to Draw a Self-Portrait
② Paintings from the 16th Century
③ A Creative Way to Make Portraits
④ The True Beauty of Renaissance Art
⑤ Why Artists Love to Draw Vegetables

2 글의 (a)~(e) 중, 전체 흐름과 <u>관계없는</u> 문장은?

① (a)　　　② (b)　　　③ (c)　　　④ (d)　　　⑤ (e)

3 <채소 기르는 사람(The Vegetable Gardener)>에 관한 글의 내용과 일치하면 T, 그렇지 않으면 F를 쓰시오.

(1) 16세기 화가의 작품이다. ___________

(2) 버섯으로 코를 표현했다. ___________

4 다음 빈칸에 알맞은 단어를 글에서 찾아 쓰시오.

> Giuseppe Arcimboldo made ___________ by painting random items.

Knowledge Bank　주세페 아르침볼도 (Giuseppe Arcimboldo, 1527~1593)

르네상스 시대에 태어난 이탈리아 출신의 화가로, 다양한 사물을 그려 사람의 얼굴을 표현하는 독특한 화풍으로 유명하다. 그는 프라하로 가서 페르디난트 1세, 막시밀리안 2세, 루돌프 2세까지 총 3대의 황제를 섬기는 궁정화가로 활동했으며 황제의 총애를 받아 귀족 작위까지 받았다. 생전에 그의 작품은 유럽을 중심으로 큰 인기를 얻었으나, 사후에 미술사에서 잊혔다. 그러나 20세기에 들어 피카소, 달리 등 초현실주의 화가들에게 영향을 주었다.

Words　**boring** ⓗ 지루한　**playful** ⓗ 장난기 많은; *재미있는, 우스꽝스러운　**portrait** ⓝ 초상화　**from a distance** 멀리서, 멀리 떨어져서　**look like** ~처럼 보이다　**be made of** ~로 만들어지다　**such as** 예를 들어, ~와 같은　**example** ⓝ 예, 사례　**vegetable** ⓝ 채소　**healthy** ⓗ 건강한; *건강에 좋은　**upside down** 거꾸로　**fat** ⓗ 뚱뚱한　**cheek** ⓝ 볼, 뺨　**lip** ⓝ 입술

문제　**self-portrait** ⓝ 자화상　**creative** ⓗ 창조적인, 창의적인　**beauty** ⓝ 아름다움, 미　**random** ⓗ 무작위의

Review Test

1-6 다음 사진에 알맞은 단어를 보기에서 골라 쓰시오.

보기 | player   cover   potter   throw   upside down   vegetable

1 

2 

3 

4 

5 

6 

7-9 다음 각 단어에 해당하는 의미를 짝지으시오.

7 creative •   • ⓐ clean and tidy

8 neat •   • ⓑ good at making new ideas

9 origin •   • ⓒ where something comes from

10-11 다음 밑줄 친 단어와 반대 의미의 단어를 고르시오.

10 My cat ate a lot and got <u>fat</u>.

① boring   ② neat   ③ thin   ④ healthy   ⑤ huge

11 The players are tired, so they might <u>lose</u> the game.

① grow   ② invent   ③ drop   ④ kneel   ⑤ win

12-14 다음 우리말과 일치하도록 빈칸에 알맞은 표현을 쓰시오.

12 The language ___________ made communication difficult.

언어 장벽은 의사소통을 어렵게 만들었다.

13 She watched the concert ___________ ___________ ___________.

그녀는 멀리서 콘서트를 보았다.

14 The kids were running ___________ ___________ ___________ in the yard.

아이들은 마당에서 왔다 갔다 뛰어다니고 있었다.

15-17 우리말과 같은 뜻이 되도록 주어진 말을 바르게 배열하시오.

15 아래로 내려갈 마지막 신체 부위는 턱이다.
(the chin, go down, the, body part, to, is, final)

→ _______________________________

16 당신은 당신의 초상화에 어떤 사물을 사용하겠는가?
(your, which, use, items, would, portrait, for, you)

→ _______________________________

17 이는 차를 즐기는 것을 어렵게 만들었다.
(difficult, this, enjoying, made, tea)

→ _______________________________

뉴욕의 아이콘 브루클린 다리

다음 두 그림을 보고 다른 곳 다섯 군데를 찾아 동그라미 하세요.

미국 뉴욕에 위치한 브루클린 다리는 맨해튼과 브루클린을 연결하며, 그 길이가 1,825m에 이릅니다. 브루클린 다리는 공학자 존 A. 로블링에 의해 설계되었고 1869년부터 15년에 걸쳐 완성되었는데, 무려 600여 명의 인부가 투입되었다고 합니다. 다리의 1층은 차도, 2층은 인도로 구성되어 있고, 걸어서 40분 정도면 다리를 건널 수 있습니다. 특히 일몰 시간에는 이곳에서 노을 지는 하늘의 환상적인 광경을 볼 수 있다고 해요.

SECTION
05

1

Every fingerprint is unique. Each dog's *nose print is unique too! Look at a dog's nose closely. You can see lines. They can help us ____________ lost dogs. In Canada, people already use these patterns to identify dogs.

Tags and collars are often used, but they can be lost or stolen. Some owners also use microchips. They are put inside dogs. This can hurt them. Microchips can also break. (a) So, many people think nose prints are better. (b) Dogs have more sensitive noses than humans. (c) Dogs' nose prints don't change as dogs get older. (d) They can't be removed either! (e) Also it's easy and painless to collect nose prints. So, dog owners, hurry up and register them!

*nose print 비문(鼻纹: 동물의 코 주름 무늬)

Think!
강아지를
잃어버리면 어떻게
찾을 수 있을까요?

114 words

1 글의 제목으로 가장 알맞은 것은?

① Lost Dogs in Canada
② Why Can Dogs Smell Well?
③ How to Register a Dog's Nose Print
④ Why Microchips Are Good for Dogs
⑤ Nose Prints: The Best Way to Identify Dogs

2 글의 빈칸에 들어갈 말로 가장 알맞은 것은?

① walk   ② find   ③ avoid
④ raise   ⑤ remember

3 글의 (a)~(e) 중, 전체 흐름과 관계<u>없는</u> 문장은?

① (a)   ② (b)   ③ (c)   ④ (d)   ⑤ (e)

서술형

4 다음 빈칸에 알맞은 단어를 보기 에서 골라 쓰시오.

| 보기 | unique   change   same   hurt |

How to Identify Dogs

Tags and Collars	Microchips	Nose Prints
They can get lost easily.	They can ⁽¹⁾__________ dogs when they are put inside dogs.	They are ⁽²⁾__________ to each dog. They are easy to collect.

Words fingerprint ⑲지문 unique ⑱유일무이한, 독특한 lost ⑱잃어버린(lose ⑧잃어버리다(lose-lost-lost))
pattern ⑲양식; *무늬 identify ⑧(신원을) 확인하다 tag ⑲꼬리표 collar ⑲(옷의) 깃; *(개 등의 목에 거는) 목걸이
steal ⑧훔치다, 도둑질하다(steal-stole-stolen) owner ⑲주인 hurt ⑧다치게 하다, 아프게 하다 break ⑧깨어지다, 부서지다
sensitive ⑱세심한; *민감한 remove ⑧제거하다 either ⑪~도 그렇다 painless ⑱고통 없는, 아프지 않은 collect ⑧모으다, 수집하다
register ⑧등록하다 문제 walk ⑧걷다; *산책시키다 avoid ⑧피하다 raise ⑧들어 올리다; *기르다

2

93 words

Do you think all superstitions are silly? Well, some started for good reasons! Take this superstition for example: you should never whistle in a theater. A long time ago, theater backgrounds were large paintings. *Stagehands raised and lowered them with ropes. To tell each other to pull or loosen the ropes, they whistled. Whistles from the audience sometimes confused them! The background could be dropped onto an actor. Ouch!

These days stagehands use headsets. Whistles don't cause accidents any more. However, the custom ______________. This is why you should not whistle at the theater.

*stagehand 무대 담당자

1 글의 주제로 가장 알맞은 것은?

① 근거 없는 미신과 관습
② 무대 담당자의 다양한 역할
③ 과거의 무대 배경 장식 방법
④ 극장에 관한 한 미신의 유래
⑤ 극장에서 발생하는 다양한 사고

고난도

2 글의 빈칸에 들어갈 말로 가장 알맞은 것은?

① starts　　② matters　　③ remains　　④ changes　　⑤ disappears

3 글의 내용과 일치하면 T, 그렇지 않으면 F를 쓰시오.

(1) 과거에는 커다란 그림이 극장의 배경으로 사용되었다.　　____________

(2) 오늘날 무대 담당자들은 헤드폰을 통해 의사소통한다.　　____________

서술형

4 다음 빈칸에 알맞은 단어를 **보기**에서 골라 쓰시오.

> **보기** │ superstition　　backgrounds　　audience　　whistles

> One ____________ says that we should not whistle in the theater.
> That's because stagehands used ____________ as signals.

3

95 words

Most cities are crowded. There is little space for trees and plants on the ground. But cities need plants and trees. They clean the air. They also prevent flooding by absorbing rain. Sometimes, they provide homes for animals and help people relax. (①) So people in cities have found a new place for plants and trees — high above their heads. (②) Architects are now designing buildings with outdoor gardens. (③) Hundreds of plants and trees can be grown in these gardens. (④) One of the most famous green buildings is in Milan, Italy. (⑤) Its name means "the vertical forest."

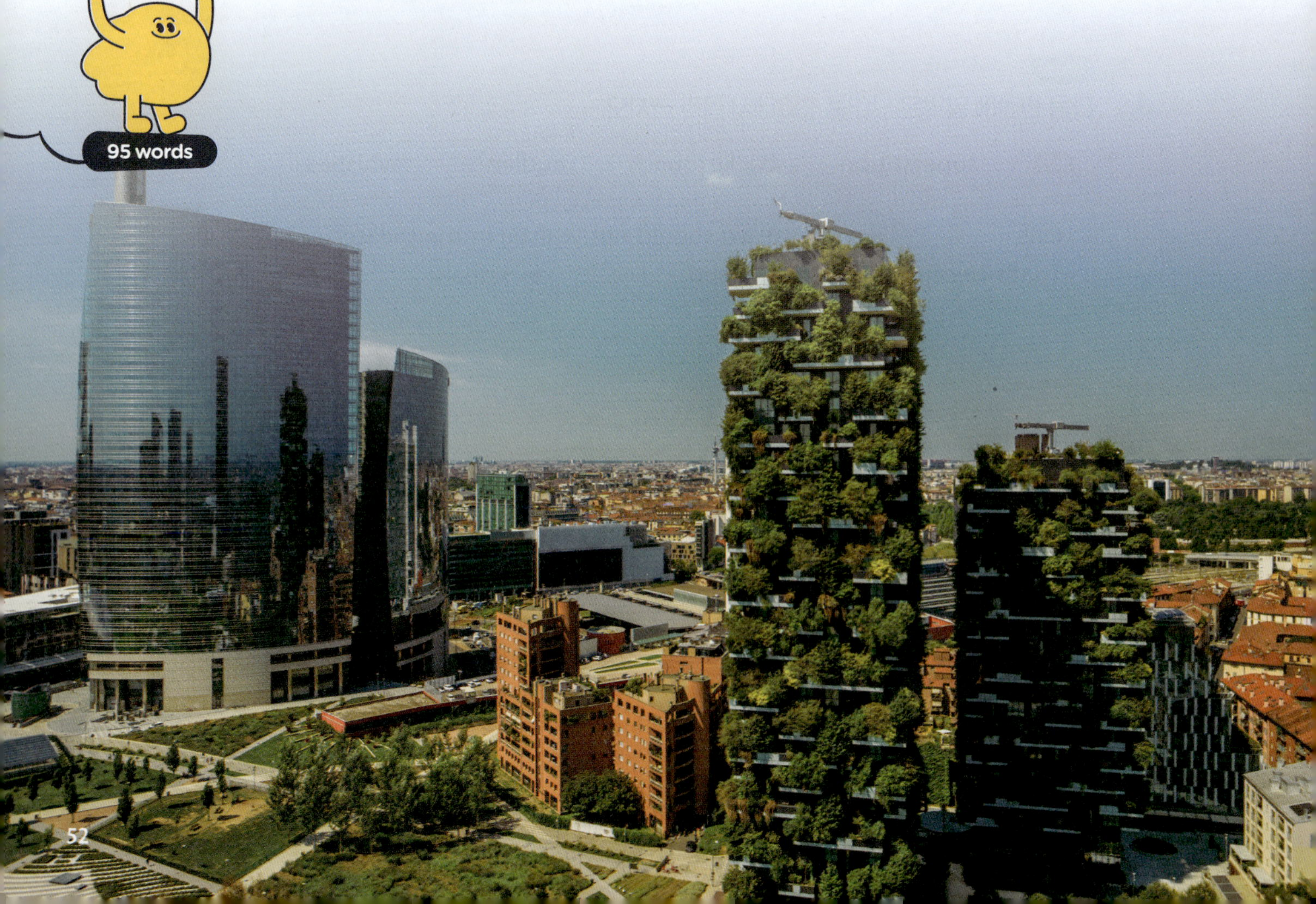

1 글의 제목으로 가장 알맞은 것은?

① What Makes Forests Disappear
② Gardens High Above the Ground
③ Protecting Forests Near Big Cities
④ Vertical Forests: Indoor Gardening
⑤ Underground Farms in Urban Areas

2 글에서 식물과 나무가 하는 일로 언급되지 <u>않은</u> 것은?

① 공기를 깨끗하게 하기
② 빗물을 흡수해서 홍수 막기
③ 바람으로부터 건물 보호하기
④ 동물들에게 서식지 제공하기
⑤ 사람들이 휴식하도록 돕기

3 다음 문장이 들어갈 위치로 가장 알맞은 곳은?

> It is called Bosco Verticale.

①   ②   ③   ④   ⑤

서술형

4 다음 빈칸에 알맞은 단어를 글에서 찾아 쓰시오.

> Because cities have little space on the __________ for plants and trees, architects are designing buildings with outdoor __________.

Words crowded 휑 붐비는   space 몡 공간   ground 몡 땅바닥; *땅   prevent 동 막다   flooding 몡 홍수   absorb 동 흡수하다
home 몡 집; *서식지   relax 동 휴식을 취하다   architect 몡 건축가   design 동 디자인[설계]하다   building 몡 건물
outdoor 휑 옥외[야외]의(↔ indoor 휑 실내의)   garden 몡 뜰, 정원   hundreds of 수백의   famous 휑 유명한   vertical 휑 수직의
문제 underground 휑 지하의   urban 휑 도시의

Review Test

 다음 사진에 알맞은 단어를 보기에서 골라 쓰시오.

보기 │ theater tag garden audience fingerprint flooding

1 

____

2 

____

3 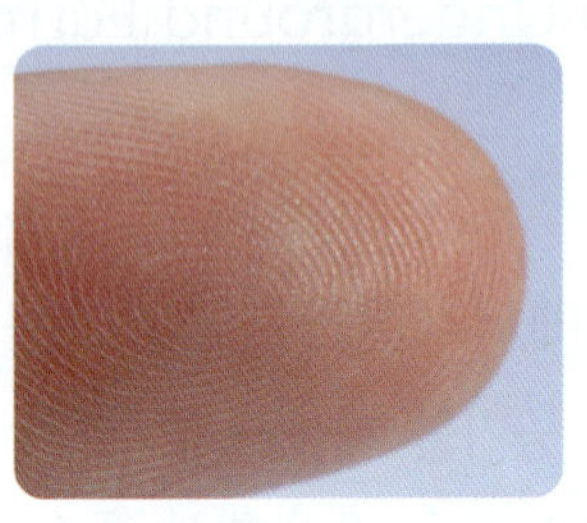

____

4 

____

5 

____

6 

____

7-9 다음 각 단어에 해당하는 의미를 짝지으시오.

7 architect •　　　• ⓐ without any pain

8 loosen •　　　• ⓑ to make something less tight

9 painless •　　　• ⓒ a person who designs buildings

10-11 다음 밑줄 친 단어와 반대 의미의 단어를 고르시오.

10 We went on an <u>outdoor</u> picnic in the park.

① sensitive　② good　③ silly　④ indoor　⑤ unique

11 Please <u>raise</u> your hand if you have a question.

① lower　② identify　③ hurt　④ remove　⑤ collect

12-14 다음 우리말과 일치하도록 빈칸에 알맞은 표현을 쓰시오.

12 _____________ _____________ people attended the concert.
수백 명의 사람들이 그 콘서트에 참석했다.

13 I need to _____________ for the online course.
나는 그 온라인 강좌에 등록해야 한다.

14 _____________ _____________, people use smartphones for everything.
오늘날 사람들은 모든 일에 스마트폰을 사용한다.

15-17 우리말과 같은 뜻이 되도록 주어진 말을 바르게 배열하시오.

15 또한 비문을 채취하는 것은 쉽고 고통이 없다.
(collect, and, painless, it's, nose prints, to, easy)

→ Also ____.

16 휘파람은 더 이상 사고를 일으키지 않는다.
(any, whistles, cause, more, don't, accidents)

→ ____

17 땅 위에 나무와 식물을 위한 공간이 거의 없다.
(there, trees and plants, space, little, is, for)

→ ____ on the ground.

영원한 사랑의 증거, 타지마할

다음 실선을 따라 한 선으로 타지마할을 그려보세요.

타지마할은 인도의 대표적 이슬람 건축물로, 무굴 제국의 황제 샤 자한이 사랑하는 아내를 추모하기 위해 지었다고 합니다. 22년 만에 완공된 이 건축물은 '찬란한 무덤'으로 불리기도 하는데요. 태양의 각도와 빛에 따라 하루에도 몇 번씩 빛깔이 달라져 시시각각 다양한 매력을 풍깁니다. 낮에는 햇빛에 하얗게 빛나고, 해가 질 무렵에는 노을에 붉게 물든 금빛을 띠며, 보름달이 뜨면 몽환적인 분위기를 연출합니다. 순백의 대리석과 수많은 보석으로 지어져 화려한 아름다움을 자랑하며, 완벽한 대칭을 뽐내는 타지마할은 유네스코 세계문화유산으로 등재되어 있답니다.

SECTION
06

1 Origins
후~ 생일 축하해

2 Health
앗, 뜨거워!

3 Mysteries
고래가 나타났다!

1

Cake with candles is a fun birthday tradition. But how did it begin? Cake with candles dates back to ancient Greece. The ancient Greeks were probably the first to put candles on cake. They gave gifts to Artemis, the goddess of the moon. (①) They gave her small cakes with candles. (②) The candles ⁵ made the cakes glow like the moon. (③) Some people believed that smoke from candles carried prayers to heaven.

(④) In the 1700s they started celebrating children's birthdays with cake. (⑤) (A) <u>Parents served a cake with the same number of candles as the child's age plus one.</u> It represented the parents' hope for their children to live longer.

Think!
생일에 어떤 소원을 빌었나요?

107 words

Knowledge Bank 고대 로마의 생일

고대 로마에서 생일은 크게 세 가지 유형으로 나뉜다. 첫 번째 유형은 가족과 친구들과 함께 보내는 사적인 생일이다. 두 번째 유형은 현재와 과거의 황제들을 위한 생일인데, 당시 살아있는 황제뿐만 아니라 죽은 황제를 위해서도 잔치를 열었다고 한다. 마지막으로 한 사람의 50번째 생일을 특별하게 기념했는데, 밀가루, 강판에 간 치즈, 올리브오일, 그리고 꿀로 만든 케이크로 생일을 축하했다고 한다.

1 글의 주제로 가장 알맞은 것은?

① 고대 그리스의 미신
② 달의 여신 아르테미스
③ 생일 케이크 초의 유래
④ 세계 각국의 생일 풍습
⑤ 장수를 비는 독일의 풍습

2 다음 문장이 들어갈 위치로 가장 알맞은 곳은?

> However, Germans probably made cake with candles a birthday tradition.

①　　　　　②　　　　　③　　　　　④　　　　　⑤

3 글의 내용과 일치하면 T, 그렇지 않으면 F를 쓰시오.

(1) 고대 그리스인들은 달의 여신에게 선물을 바쳤다. ___________

(2) 고대 그리스인들은 연기가 기도를 하늘에 전한다고 믿었다. ___________

고난도

4 글에 따르면, 밑줄 친 (A)의 이유는?

① 독일인들이 큰 숫자를 좋아해서
② 신에게 초 하나를 바치기 위해서
③ 아이들이 더 오래 살기를 희망해서
④ 케이크를 더 예쁘게 장식하기 위해서
⑤ 더 많은 초를 끄는 즐거움을 주기 위해서

Words　candle ⑱ 초, 양초　tradition ⑱ 전통　begin ⑧ 시작되다[하다]　date back to ~까지 거슬러 올라가다　ancient ⑱ 고대의
Greek ⑱ 그리스인　probably ⑨ 아마　first ⑱ 최초의 인물　goddess ⑱ 여신　glow ⑧ 빛나다　smoke ⑱ 연기
carry ⑧ 나르다, 전하다　prayer ⑱ 기도　celebrate ⑧ 기념하다, 축하하다　serve ⑧ 제공하다, 차려 주다　the number of ~의 수
represent ⑧ 대표하다; *나타내다, 표현하다　hope ⑱ 희망

2

Think!

화상을 입어본 적이
있나요? 어떻게
대처했나요?

99 words

In the kitchen, you burn your hand on a hot pan. You run to get some ice to ease the pain. Stop! Ice doesn't help.

(①) Some scientists compared the treatment effects of ice and other cures. (②) Also, ice caused *frostbite and the most serious skin damage. (③)

So, how can we treat a burn? (④) Put the burn under cool, running water for 20 minutes. (⑤) Or you can use a cool, wet cloth. Then clean the area. In this way, you can treat most minor burns at home. However, see a doctor if your skin doesn't get better in two weeks.

*frostbite 동상

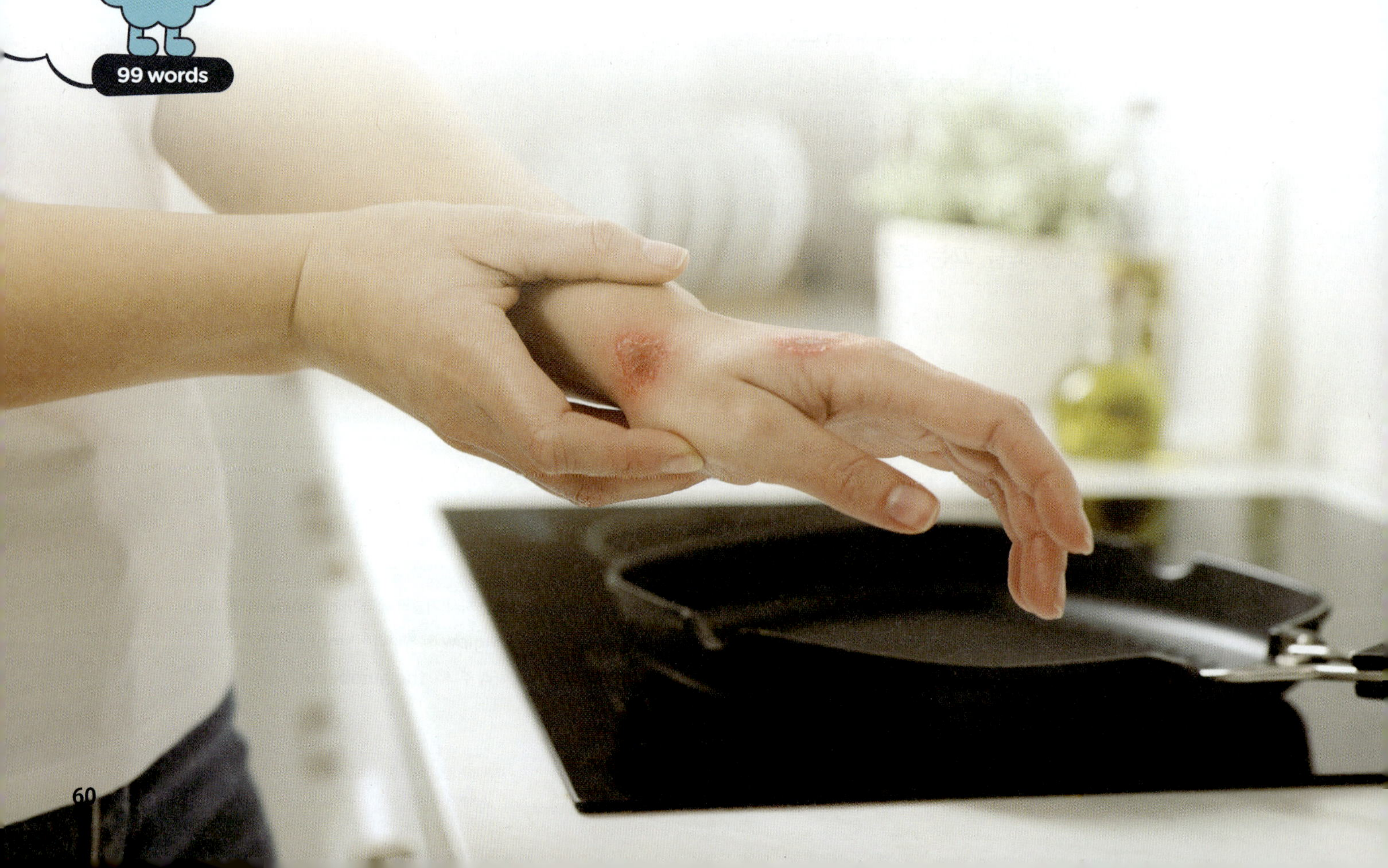

1 글의 주제로 가장 알맞은 것은?

① use of ice for treatment
② simple ways to ease pain
③ how to take care of your skin
④ why you shouldn't put ice on burns
⑤ why you should be careful in the kitchen

2 다음 문장이 들어갈 위치로 가장 알맞은 곳은?

> They found ice actually made the burn get better more slowly.

①   ②   ③   ④   ⑤

3 글의 내용과 일치하면 T, 그렇지 않으면 F를 쓰시오.

(1) 화상을 입은 곳에 얼음을 가져다 대면 피부가 손상될 수 있다.　＿＿＿＿＿＿＿

(2) 화상이 2주 이상 지속될 경우, 집에서 치료할 수 있다.　＿＿＿＿＿＿＿

서술형

4 다음 빈칸에 알맞은 단어를 글에서 찾아 쓰시오.

> When you get a ＿＿＿＿＿＿, you should not put ＿＿＿＿＿＿ on it.
> Instead, put it under cool, running water.

SECTION 06

3

Think!

명화의 숨겨진
비밀에 대해서 들어본
적이 있나요?

113 words

One *restorer was cleaning a 17th-century painting. It was made by Dutch painter Hendrick van Anthonissen. The painting was a scene of people on a beach. But it had a secret. As she cleaned the painting, a thin layer of paint came off. She saw something strange. Surprisingly, it was a 5 huge fin! She continued to remove the layers of paint. Soon a dead whale appeared on the beach.

But why was the whale hidden? Researchers said dead whales were an unpleasant subject for the people of that time. Some people believed they meant ______________. So it 10 is likely that the whale was covered up. But that's just one guess. We may never know!

*restorer (예술 작품 등의) 복원 전문가

1 글의 주제로 가장 알맞은 것은?

① 17세기 미술의 특징

② 그림을 복원하는 과정

③ 고래가 숨어있던 한 그림

④ 고래가 해변에서 죽는 이유

⑤ 해변을 주제로 하는 다양한 작품

2 그림에 관한 글의 내용과 일치하지 <u>않는</u> 것은?

① 17세기에 그려졌다.

② 네덜란드의 화가에 의해 그려졌다.

③ 해변에서 그려진 것으로 알려져 있다.

④ 복원 전문가는 그림을 닦다가 이상한 점을 발견했다.

⑤ 그림이 그려질 당시 죽은 고래는 불쾌한 대상으로 여겨졌다.

서술형

3 글의 밑줄 친 <u>a secret</u>이 의미하는 내용을 우리말로 쓰시오.

____

4 글의 빈칸에 들어갈 말로 가장 알맞은 것은?

① peace　　　　② power　　　　③ victory

④ bad luck　　　⑤ a long life

Words　Dutch ⑱ 네덜란드의, 네덜란드인의　scene ⑲ 현장; *장면, 광경　beach ⑲ 해변, 바닷가　thin ⑱ 얇은, 가는　layer ⑲ 막, 층, 겹　come off 떼어지다, 떨어지다　strange ⑱ 이상한　surprisingly ⑤ 놀랍게도　huge ⑱ 거대한　fin ⑲ 지느러미　continue ⑧ 계속하다[되다]　remove ⑧ 제거하다, 없애다　dead ⑱ 죽은　whale ⑲ 고래　appear ⑧ 나타나다　hide ⑧ 감추다, 숨기다(hide-hid-hidden)　unpleasant ⑱ 불쾌한　subject ⑲ 주제, 대상　likely ⑱ 가능성 있는, ~할 것 같은　cover up ~을 완전히 덮다[가리다]　guess ⑲ 추측, 짐작　문제 peace ⑲ 평화　victory ⑲ 승리　bad luck 불운

Review Test

1-6 다음 사진에 알맞은 단어를 [보기]에서 골라 쓰시오.

[보기]   pan   hide   smoke   whale   cloth   candle

1 ________________

2 ________________

3 ________________

4 ________________

5 ________________

6 ________________

7-9 다음 각 단어에 해당하는 의미를 짝지으시오.

7   carry •   • ⓐ no longer alive

8   ease •   • ⓑ to move something from one place to another

9   dead •   • ⓒ to make something better or less painful

10-11 다음 밑줄 친 단어와 반대 의미의 단어를 고르시오.

10   The injury looked very <u>serious</u>.

    ① bad   ② minor   ③ similar   ④ likely   ⑤ important

11   This room has an <u>unpleasant</u> smell.

    ① nice   ② smelly   ③ strange   ④ unique   ⑤ familiar

12-14 다음 우리말과 일치하도록 빈칸에 알맞은 표현을 쓰시오.

12 I hope you _____________ _____________ soon.
나는 네가 곧 낫기를 바란다.

13 The history of ancient Egypt _____________ _____________ _____________ 6000 B.C.
고대 이집트의 역사는 기원전 6000년으로 거슬러 올라간다.

14 The sticker won't _____________ _____________ the wall.
그 스티커는 벽에서 떨어지지 않을 것이다.

15-17 우리말과 같은 뜻이 되도록 주어진 말을 바르게 배열하시오.

15 그녀는 물감의 겹들을 계속해서 제거했다.
(the layers, continued, she, of, to, paint, remove)

→ ____

16 그것은 아이들이 더 오래 살기를 바라는 부모의 바람을 나타냈다.
(to, their children, live, represented, the parent's hope, it, longer, for)

→ ____

17 몇몇 과학자들이 얼음과 다른 치료법의 치료 효과를 비교했다.
(some scientists, the treatment effects, ice, compared, other cures, and, of)

→ ____

아름답고 거대한 보물 창고
루브르 박물관

다음 그림에 숨겨진 물건들을 찾아보세요.

숨은 그림 티셔츠, 포크, 공책, 옷걸이, 칫솔

프랑스 파리에 있는 루브르 박물관은 세계 3대 박물관입니다. 매년 가장 많은 관람객이 방문하는 세계 최대 규모의 박물관으로, 파리에 가면 꼭 방문해 보아야 할 명소입니다. 정문에는 루브르의 상징으로 여겨지는 유리 피라미드가 아름다움을 뽐내고 있습니다. 루브르 박물관에서는 레오나르도 다빈치의 〈모나리자〉와 조각상 〈밀로의 비너스〉를 비롯하여 3만 점이 넘는 명작을 볼 수 있답니다.

SECTION
07

1

119 words

You get on a flight and put on your seat belt. You want to get some sleep. But sleeping during takeoff and landing is not a good idea. 5

At these times, the air pressure in the airplane changes quickly. This changes the pressure in your ears. Your ears may *pop. To reduce the pressure in your ears, you can yawn or swallow. Chewing gum helps, too. (a) But you cannot do these things when you are asleep. (b) This could damage your ears. (c) You 10 might feel dizzy. (d) At worst you could lose some of your hearing. (e) Listening to loud music might lead to hearing loss.

So next time you feel sleepy on an airplane, remember: be awake during takeoff and landing.

*pop (기압 변화로 귀가) 먹먹해지다

1 글의 주제로 가장 알맞은 것은?

① 비행기에서 귀가 먹먹한 이유

② 비행기에서 숙면할 수 있는 방법

③ 비행기에서 지켜야 할 안전 수칙

④ 잦은 비행이 귀 건강에 미치는 영향

⑤ 비행기 이착륙 시 자면 안 되는 이유

2 글의 (a)~(e) 중, 전체 흐름과 관계<u>없는</u> 문장은?

① (a)　　　② (b)　　　③ (c)　　　④ (d)　　　⑤ (e)

3 글에서 귀 내부의 압력을 낮추기 위한 방법으로 언급된 것을 <u>모두</u> 고르시오.

① 하품하기　　　② 혀 내밀기　　　③ 침 삼키기

④ 고개 숙이기　　　⑤ 껌 씹기

4 다음 빈칸에 알맞은 단어를 글에서 찾아 쓰시오.

> You need to be ___________ during takeoff and landing. You cannot do anything to reduce the pressure in your ears when you are ___________.

Words　flight 몡 비행; *항공기　put on ~을 입다, 착용하다　seat belt 몡 안전띠　sleep 몡 잠, 수면 통 (잠을) 자다(sleepy 혱 졸음이 오는)　takeoff 몡 이륙　landing 몡 착륙　pressure 몡 압력　airplane 몡 비행기　reduce 통 줄이다, 낮추다　yawn 통 하품하다　swallow 통 침을 삼키다　chew 통 (음식을) 씹다　asleep 혱 잠이 든　damage 통 손상을 주다　dizzy 혱 어지러운　lose 통 잃다, 상실하다(loss 몡 상실, 손실)　hearing 몡 청력, 청각　loud 혱 소리가 큰, 시끄러운　lead to ~로 이어지다　awake 혱 깨어 있는

Whistles are useful for referees. But they didn't always have ⓐ <u>them</u>. At first, they waved flags and shouted to get players' attention. (①) Shouting was fine for small games. (②) The crowds became bigger and louder. (③) In the noise, players couldn't hear the referees. (④) Referees really needed something! (⑤)

Inventor Joseph Hudson gave ⓑ <u>them</u> a solution. He invented a new whistle in the 1880s. It was for the police at first, but later he introduced it to sports. It could be heard in large crowds. It was much better than shouting! Soon, the whistle became common.

Now whistles are used in most noisy sports, and even in the Olympics.

Knowledge Bank 심판에서 발명가로

캐나다 출신의 심판이었던 론 폭스크로프트(Ron Foxcroft)는 1976년 몬트리올 올림픽 농구 결승전에서 반칙 선언을 하기 위해 호루라기를 불었다. 하지만 호루라기가 울리지 않아 관중들로부터 큰 비난을 받았고 결국 심판을 그만두기에 이르렀다. 이후에 그는 세게 불면 소리가 나지 않거나 쉽게 고장이 나는 기존 호루라기의 문제점들을 보완한 새로운 호루라기를 개발하였다. 그의 호루라기는 1.6㎞가 넘는 거리에서도 잘 들렸다. 그가 개발한 호루라기는 세계 정상급 대회는 물론 인명구조 현장에서도 사용되고 있다.

1 글의 제목으로 가장 알맞은 것은?

① When Is a Whistle Used?
② Referees: The Sports Police
③ The Use of Whistles in Sports
④ Useful Inventions for the Police
⑤ Problems with Crowds at Stadiums

서술형

2 글의 밑줄 친 ⓐ와 ⓑ가 각각 가리키는 것을 글에서 찾아 쓰시오.

ⓐ: _______________________   ⓑ: _______________________

3 다음 문장이 들어갈 위치로 가장 알맞은 곳은?

> But in the 19th century, sports became popular.

①   ②   ③   ④   ⑤

4 글의 내용과 일치하면 T, 그렇지 않으면 F를 쓰시오.

(1) Joseph Hudson이 발명한 호루라기는 처음에 경찰을 위한 것이었다. _______

(2) 경찰이 스포츠 심판에게 호루라기를 도입하게 했다. _______

Words   whistle ⑲호각, 호루라기   useful ⑲유용한   referee ⑲심판   not always 항상 ~인 것은 아니다   wave ⑧흔들다
flag ⑲깃발   shout ⑧외치다, 소리치다   attention ⑲주의, 주목   crowd ⑲사람들, 군중   noise ⑲소음(noisy ⑲시끄러운)
inventor ⑲발명가(invent ⑧발명하다)   solution ⑲해결책   introduce ⑧(사람을) 소개하다; *내놓다, 도입하다   common ⑲흔한
문제 stadium ⑲경기장   popular ⑲인기 있는

3

Think!
맛있는 음식을
먹을 때 어떤
기분이 드나요?

108 words

We feel happy when we eat delicious food. Gorillas do too, and they show it!

*Zoologist Eva Luef studied wild gorillas in the Congo. She found that they made two different sounds during meals. One sound was a deep, steady humming. It sounded like a sigh of **satisfaction. The other sound was like a song. Gorillas sang different notes to make their own melody. Each gorilla has its own style. You can tell who is singing. Their songs might tell others to come and enjoy the food with them. When they have their favorite food, they sing more loudly! These two habits are ways to show their happiness.

*zoologist 동물학자   **satisfaction 만족

1 글의 제목으로 가장 알맞은 것은?

① Can Gorillas Sing?
② Do Gorillas Have Feelings Too?
③ Delicious Food Makes Gorillas Sing!
④ Eva Luef: The Best Zoologist in History
⑤ Differences between Humans and Gorillas

2 글의 내용과 일치하면 T, 그렇지 않으면 F를 쓰시오.

(1) Eva Luef는 콩고의 동물원에 있는 고릴라를 연구했다. ＿＿＿＿＿

(2) 고릴라는 각자 자신만의 노래 스타일을 가지고 있다. ＿＿＿＿＿

서술형

3 다음 질문에 우리말로 답하시오.

> Q: What do gorillas do when they eat their favorite food?

＿＿＿＿＿＿＿＿＿＿＿＿＿＿＿＿＿＿＿＿＿＿＿＿＿＿＿＿＿＿＿＿

서술형

4 다음 빈칸에 알맞은 단어를 보기에서 골라 쓰시오.

| 보기 | happy | sleep | eat | hungry |

> Gorillas make two sounds when they ＿＿＿＿＿. These sounds show that they are ＿＿＿＿＿.

Words

delicious 형 아주 맛있는　show 동 보여 주다　wild 형 야생의　meal 명 식사　deep 형 깊은; *낮은, 저음의
steady 형 고정적인, 한결같은　humming 명 콧노래　sound like ~처럼 들리다　sigh 명 한숨, 탄식　note 명 메모; *음조, 음
own 형 자신의　tell 동 말하다; 구별하다　favorite 형 매우 좋아하는　loudly 부 큰 소리로　habit 명 습관　문제 feeling 명 느낌; *pl. 감정
history 명 역사　difference 명 차이, 차이점

Review Test

1-6 다음 사진에 알맞은 단어를 보기 에서 골라 쓰시오.

보기 | yawn   whistle   flight   meal   sigh   stadium

1

2

3

4

5

6

7-9 다음 각 단어에 해당하는 의미를 짝지으시오.

7 crowd •   • ⓐ to make something new

8 invent •   • ⓑ not changing over time

9 steady •   • ⓒ a large number of people in the same place

10-11 다음 밑줄 친 단어와 반대 의미의 단어를 고르시오.

10 Please turn off your cell phones during <u>takeoff</u>.

① trip   ② flight   ③ landing   ④ stadium   ⑤ humming

11 The classroom was <u>noisy</u> during the break.

① quiet   ② common   ③ popular   ④ useful   ⑤ wild

12-14 다음 우리말과 일치하도록 빈칸에 알맞은 표현을 쓰시오.

12   The sun is bright, so ______________ ______________ sunglasses.
햇빛이 눈부시니 선글라스를 착용해라.

13   The weather is ______________ ______________ sunny.
날씨가 항상 맑은 것은 아니다.

14   This music ______________ ______________ rain.
이 음악은 빗소리처럼 들린다.

15-17 우리말과 같은 뜻이 되도록 주어진 말을 바르게 배열하시오.

15   군중이 더 많아지고 더 시끄러워졌다.
(louder, the crowds, bigger, became, and)

→ ____

16   당신은 누가 노래하고 있는지 구분할 수 있다.
(singing, you, is, can, who, tell)

→ ____

17   시끄러운 음악을 듣는 것은 청력 상실로 이어질 수도 있다.
(loud, to, hearing loss, might, listening, music, to, lead)

→ ____

브라질의 두 팔 벌린 예수상

브라질의 거대한 예수상을 자유롭게 색칠해 보세요.

예수상은 브라질 리우데자네이루의 코르코바도산 정상에 위치한 그리스도상입니다. 두 팔을 양쪽으로 활짝 뻗고 서 있는 모습의 이 조각상은 브라질이 포르투갈로부터 독립한 지 100주년이 되는 해를 기념하기 위해 만들어졌답니다. 전체 높이는 38m이며, 양팔을 뻗은 길이는 28m나 되고 무게는 1,145톤에 이릅니다. 조각상 내부에는 150명을 수용할 수 있는 예배당이 있습니다. 예수상이 있는 곳에서 내려다보는 리우데자네이루 시내의 모습이 정말 멋지다고 합니다.

SECTION
08

1

Do you love Christmas? Then you'll love Drøbak, Norway. It's Christmas all year in Drøbak! In Norway, people say that Santa Claus was born in Drøbak. You can see special street signs about Santa there. They tell you to watch out for Santa. ⁵

The village is mainly famous for Tregaarden's Julehus, or "Christmas House." You can buy Christmas decorations and candles there. Around 250,000 people visit it each year. (A) And Santa's post office is next door. ¹⁰ (B) He will read your letter during November and December. (C) You can buy stamps and send Santa a letter. If you're lucky, you can take a picture with him on Christmas Day!

Think!

산타클로스는 어디에서 태어났을까요?

107 words

Knowledge Bank 핀란드에도 산타가?

핀란드의 로바니에미에도 산타클로스가 사는 마을이 있다. 한 해에 약 40만 명의 관광객이 찾는 이 마을의 산타클로스 우체국에서는 빨간 옷을 입은 요정들이 전 세계에서 온 편지를 분류하고 12개 국어로 답장을 쓰는 일을 돕는다. 편지에 주소나 우표가 없어도 'To Santa Claus(산타클로스에게)'라고 쓰여 있으면, 이곳으로 보내진다고 한다.

1 글의 제목으로 가장 알맞은 것은?

① Who Is Santa Claus?
② The Origin of Christmas
③ A Christmas Town in Norway
④ Write a Christmas Card to Santa!
⑤ Christmas Traditions around the World

고난도

2 문장 (A)~(C)를 글의 흐름에 알맞게 배열한 것은?

① (A)-(B)-(C)　　② (A)-(C)-(B)　　③ (B)-(C)-(A)
④ (C)-(A)-(B)　　⑤ (C)-(B)-(A)

3 Drøbak 마을에 관한 글의 내용과 일치하지 <u>않는</u> 것은?

① 산타가 태어난 곳으로 알려져 있다.
② 산타를 조심하라는 표지판을 볼 수 있다.
③ 매년 약 25만 명의 사람들이 Tregaarden's Julehus에 방문한다.
④ 산타의 우체국은 Tregaarden's Julehus 옆에 위치해 있다.
⑤ 11월과 12월에 산타와 사진을 찍을 수 있다.

서술형

4 다음 빈칸에 알맞은 단어를 글에서 찾아 쓰시오.

> You can buy decorations and __________ for Christmas in Tregaarden's Julehus, and you can send a __________ to Santa at Santa's post office.

Words be born 태어나다　street ⑲ 거리, 도로　sign ⑲ 기호, 부호; *표지판　watch out for ~에 대해 주의하다
be famous for ~로 유명하다　mainly ⑼ 주로　decoration ⑲ 장식품　candle ⑲ 양초, 초　visit ⑧ 방문하다
post office ⑲ 우체국　stamp ⑲ 우표　lucky ⑳ 운이 좋은　take a picture 사진을 찍다　**문제** origin ⑲ 기원　tradition ⑲ 전통

104 words

You accidentally swallowed gum. Oops! According to some people, now it will stay in your body for seven years. Is that true?

No! Your body treats gum like any other food. First, some parts of it break down in your stomach. Then your body saves [5] any nutrients. But your body cannot digest one part: the gum base. The chemicals in the gum base don't break down easily. So your body simply pushes it through your digestive system. And finally it leaves your body.

Swallowing gum is usually harmless, but don't make it a [10] habit. Swallowing too much gum at once can cause digestive problems!

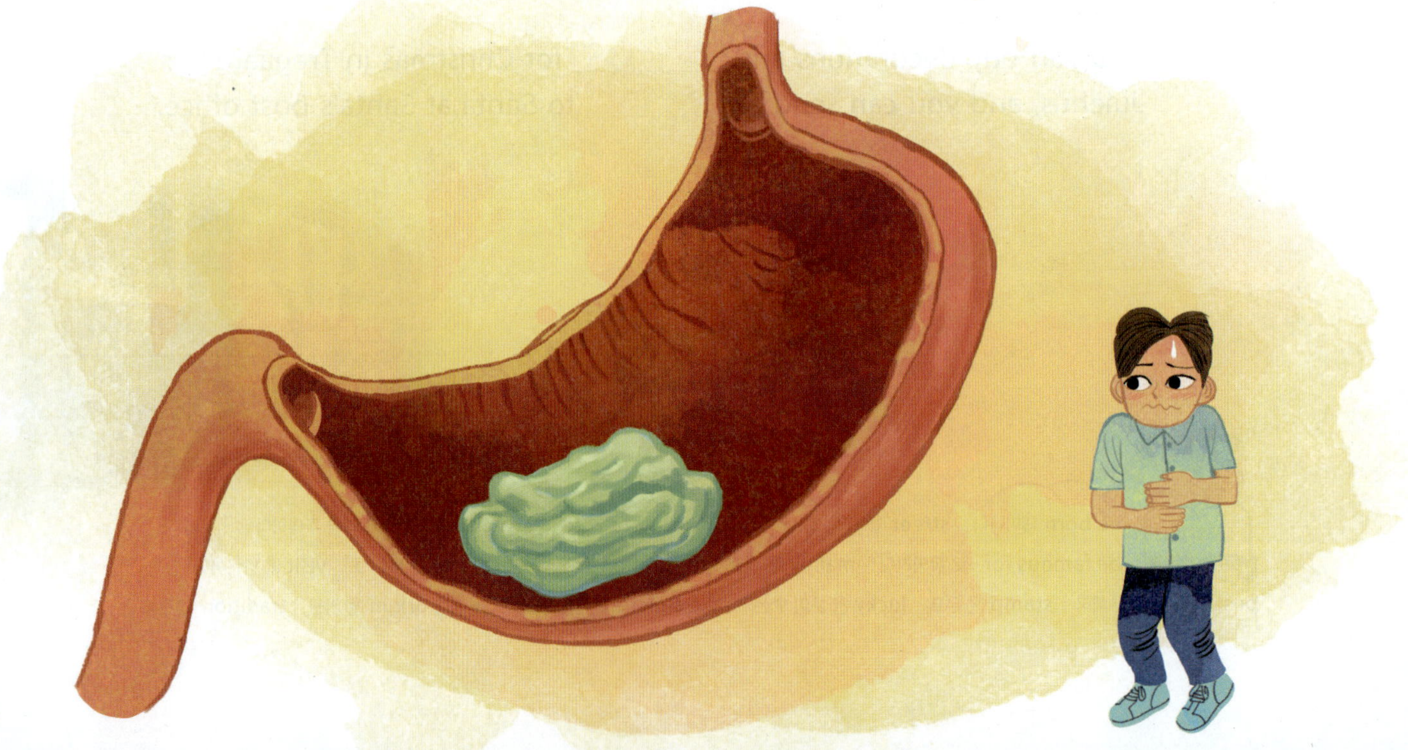

1 글의 주제로 가장 알맞은 것은?

① 껌의 영양성분
② 음식이 소화되는 과정
③ 껌을 삼키면 일어나는 일
④ 껌을 삼키면 안 되는 이유
⑤ 껌 제조에 사용되는 화학 물질

2 글의 내용과 일치하면 T, 그렇지 않으면 F를 쓰시오.

(1) 우리의 몸은 껌을 다른 음식과는 다르게 취급한다. ____________

(2) 껌 기초제 속의 화학 물질은 쉽게 소화되지 않는다. ____________

서술형

3 한꺼번에 껌을 많이 삼키면 안 되는 이유를 우리말로 쓰시오.

____

고난도 서술형

4 다음 빈칸에 알맞은 단어를 보기에서 골라 쓰시오.

보기	swallow	digest	cause	stay

When you ____________ gum, your body saves the nutrients from it. But your stomach cannot ____________ the gum base. So your body simply pushes it through.

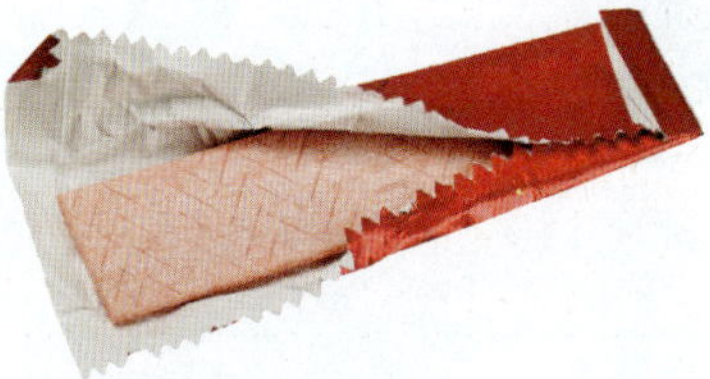

Words accidentally ㈜ 잘못하여, 뜻하지 않게 swallow ⑧ 삼키다 according to ~에 따르면 stay ⑧ 머무르다, 남다 treat ⑧ 취급하다, 대하다 part ⑲ 부분 break down 분해되다[하다] stomach ⑲ 위, 복부 save ⑧ 구하다; *저장하다 nutrient ⑲ 영양소, 영양분 digest ⑧ 소화시키다(digestive ⑱ 소화의) chemical ⑲ 화학 물질 simply ㈜ 그저, 단순히 push ⑧ 밀다, 밀어내다 leave ⑧ 떠나다 harmless ⑱ 해가 없는, 무해한 at once 한꺼번에

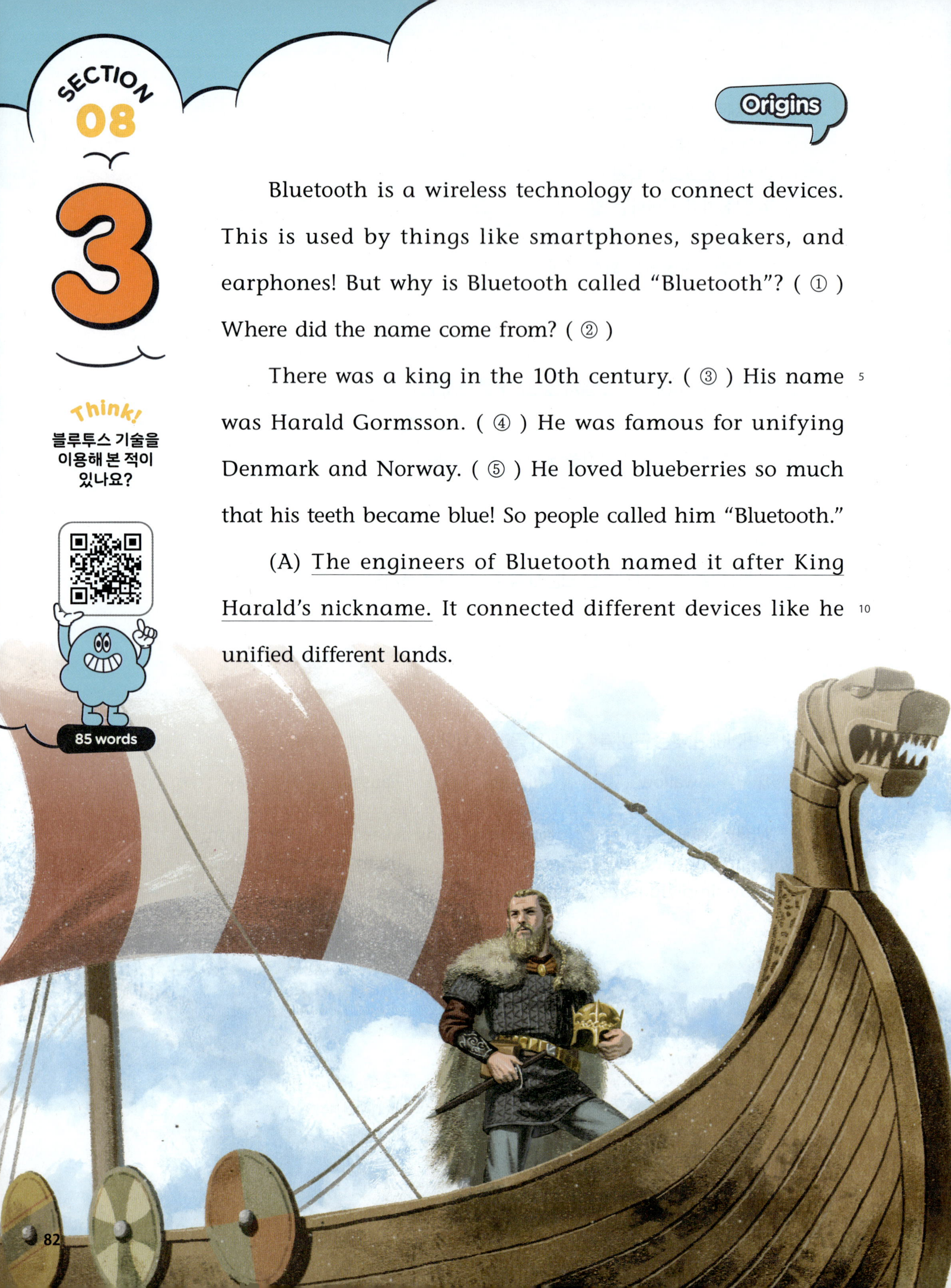

3

Bluetooth is a wireless technology to connect devices. This is used by things like smartphones, speakers, and earphones! But why is Bluetooth called "Bluetooth"? (①) Where did the name come from? (②)

There was a king in the 10th century. (③) His name was Harald Gormsson. (④) He was famous for unifying Denmark and Norway. (⑤) He loved blueberries so much that his teeth became blue! So people called him "Bluetooth."

(A) The engineers of Bluetooth named it after King Harald's nickname. It connected different devices like he unified different lands.

Think!
블루투스 기술을
이용해 본 적이
있나요?

85 words

1 글의 제목으로 가장 알맞은 것은?

① How to Connect Devices
② How Bluetooth Got Its Name
③ Bluetooth: A Useful Technology
④ Funny Nicknames of Famous Kings
⑤ Who Is the Greatest King in History?

2 다음 문장이 들어갈 위치로 가장 알맞은 곳은?

> There is an interesting story behind it.

①　　　　②　　　　③　　　　④　　　　⑤

고난도

3 글에 따르면, 밑줄 친 (A)의 이유는?

① 기술자들이 가장 존경하는 왕이어서
② 왕이 통합한 국가에서 기술이 발명되어서
③ 왕이 기술의 기본 원리를 최초로 발견해서
④ 왕이 땅을 통합한 것처럼 기술이 기기들을 연결해서
⑤ 왕의 명성을 이용하여 기술을 쉽게 홍보할 수 있어서

서술형

4 Harald 왕이 'Bluetooth'라고 불린 이유를 우리말로 쓰시오.

____

Knowledge Bank 블루투스 로고의 비밀

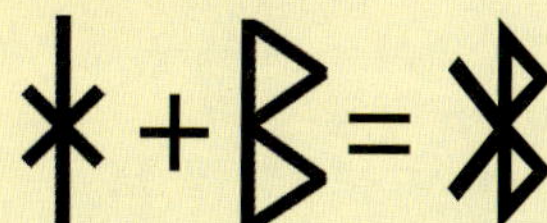

우리가 스마트폰을 비롯한 다양한 전자기기에서 흔히 볼 수 있는 블루투스의 로고는 Harald Gormsson의 이름에서 유래되었다. 그의 별명인 Harald Bluetooth의 이니셜 H, B를 스칸디나비아의 전통 문자인 룬 문자로 써서 하나로 합치면 우리가 알고 있는 블루투스의 로고가 된다.

Words   wireless 혱 무선의   technology 몡 (과학) 기술   connect 통 연결하다   device 몡 장치, 기기   come from ~에서 나오다, 비롯되다   unify 통 통합하다   engineer 몡 엔지니어, 기술자   name after ~의 이름을 따서 명명하다   nickname 몡 별명   land 몡 땅

Review Test

 다음 사진에 알맞은 단어를 보기에서 골라 쓰시오.

보기 | stamp   connect   engineer   push   stomach   sign

1 

2 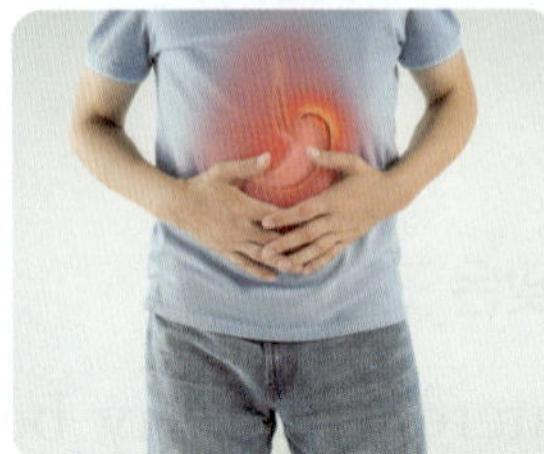

3 

4 

5 

6 

7-9 다음 각 단어에 해당하는 의미를 짝지으시오.

7 lucky • • ⓐ to make food go from your mouth to your stomach

8 swallow • • ⓑ having good fortune

9 unify • • ⓒ to bring together two or more things to make one

10-11 다음 밑줄 친 단어와 반대 의미의 단어를 고르시오.

10 Why do you want to <u>leave</u> your hometown?

① stay   ② take   ③ send   ④ visit   ⑤ choose

11 The spider looks scary, but it's <u>harmless</u>.

① favorite   ② good   ③ harmful   ④ famous   ⑤ wireless

12-14 다음 우리말과 일치하도록 빈칸에 알맞은 표현을 쓰시오.

12 The city _____________ _____________ _____________ its beautiful beaches.
그 도시는 아름다운 해변들로 유명하다.

13 _____________ _____________ the weather report, it will rain tomorrow.
일기 예보에 따르면, 내일 비가 올 것이다.

14 He decided to _____________ his dog _____________ a movie character.
그는 영화 등장인물의 이름을 따서 자신의 개의 이름을 짓기로 결정했다.

15-17 우리말과 같은 뜻이 되도록 주어진 말을 바르게 배열하시오.

15 그는 블루베리를 너무 좋아해서 치아가 파랗게 되었다!
(blueberries, loved, blue, much, became, so, his teeth, that, he)

→ ____

16 우선, 그것의 일부는 당신의 위에서 분해된다.
(some, your, down, in, break, it, stomach, of, parts)

→ First, ____.

17 그것들은 당신에게 산타를 조심하라고 말해 준다.
(they, Santa, watch, you, tell, to, out, for)

→ ____

싱가포르의 상징물이 있는 머라이언 공원

다음 두 그림을 보고 다른 곳 다섯 군데를 찾아 동그라미 하세요.

머라이어 공원은 싱가포르의 상징물인 머라이언 상이 설치되어 있는 곳으로, 싱가포르 강과 바다가 만나는 곳에 위치해 있습니다. 머라이언(Merlion)은 'mermaid(인어)'와 'lion(사자)'의 합성어로 상반신은 사자, 하반신은 물고기의 모습을 한 가상의 동물입니다. 머라이언 상은 시내 곳곳에 있는데, 그중 머라이언 공원에 있는 것의 높이는 8.6m, 무게는 70톤에 달합니다. 물을 뿜어내는 이 머라이언 상과 기념사진을 찍으러 찾아오는 관광객이 매우 많아서 관광 명소로 꼽힙니다.

Reading TUTOR 리딩튜터

Starter 2

직독직해 Worksheet

1 크래커도 숨을 쉬어요

① Crackers are a popular snack. / ② They have different flavors. /

③ There are many shapes and sizes, too. / ④ But / they have one thing

in common. / ⑤ They all have holes. / ⑥ The holes are important. / ⑦

There are air bubbles / in cracker dough. / ⑧ The dough is heated / in an

oven. / ⑨ Then the bubbles get bigger / and pop. / (⑩ Hot ovens can be

dangerous. /) ⑪ This gives crackers / a strange shape. / ⑫ So / a special

machine is used. / ⑬ It makes tiny holes / in the crackers. / ⑭ The air comes

out / through the holes. / ⑮ Finally, / the crackers stay flat / and perfect! /

2 내 빵 돌려내!

① Two cats fought for a piece of bread. / ② They both wanted it. / ③ A

smart monkey saw them / and offered to help. / ④ He said / he'd split the

bread / in half. / ⑤ The cats agreed. / ⑥ The monkey split the bread / in

half. / ⑦ One piece was bigger / than the other. / ⑧ The monkey wanted

them / to be equal. / ⑨ He took a bite / of the bigger piece. / ⑩ Now / the

other piece was bigger. / ⑪ This happened / again and again. / ⑫ Soon

/ the bread was gone. / ⑬ The monkey had a full stomach. / ⑭ The cats

didn't get anything. / ⑮ They went home hungry. /

3 아니, 무슨 냄새지?

① The world is filled / with many different smells. / ② But / what does

the rest of the galaxy smell like? / ③ Well, / scientists can tell you / about

one planet. / ④ Uranus smells like farts! / ⑤ How do they know? / ⑥ They

studied / the clouds of Uranus. / ⑦ They discovered / the clouds are made

of / hydrogen sulfide. / ⑧ This gas smells / like farts or rotten eggs. / (⑨ If

you fart too often, / you should see a doctor. /) ⑩ Don't worry / though. /

⑪ You will never smell Uranus. / ⑫ It's about -200°C there! / ⑬ Humans

can't survive / even for a second! /

⑭ Now / scientists are looking at Neptune. / ⑮ They think / it might be

covered / in a similar gas. /

1 보기보다 무시무시해

① Think of / the world's most dangerous animal. / ② Are they snakes? /

③ Sharks? Bears? / ④ The answer may surprise you. / ⑤ It is mosquitoes. /

⑥ Why are mosquitoes so dangerous? / ⑦ You might not worry / about

an itchy mosquito bite. / ⑧ But / it can become a big problem. / ⑨ Many

mosquitoes carry diseases. / ⑩ These diseases can spread / when they bite

humans. / ⑪ Such diseases can be deadly. /

⑫ So, / how can you protect yourself / from mosquitoes? / ⑬ Avoiding

mosquito bites is the best way. / ⑭ Wear a long-sleeved shirt / outside. /

⑮ Wear long pants, / too. / ⑯ Then / mosquitoes cannot bite you / easily. /

⑰ It may be hotter, / but it is safer! /

2 이 조그마한 걸 어디에 쓰지?

① Have you seen strange, tiny pockets / on your jeans? / ② You cannot

put much / in them. / ③ So, / what are they for? / ④ Well, / back in the late

1800s, / people had pocket watches! / ⑤ Workers usually put their watches

/ in their vests. / ⑥ But / their watches often fell out / and broke. /

⑦ Denim jeans company founder Levi Strauss / came up with a bright

idea: / a watch pocket! / ⑧ Workers could finally keep their watches / in a

safe place. / ⑨ Today / few people carry / pocket watches. / ⑩ However, /

the company wants / to keep the original design. / ⑪ So / the pockets have

stayed. / ⑫ The next time you see / that little pocket, / remember / it was

once useful! /

3 가장 특별한 아침 식사

① Do you love animals? / ② Then / this hotel in Nairobi, Kenya / is

for you. / ③ It is next to a protected area / with a group of Rothschild's

giraffes. / ④ These giraffes are at risk / in the wild. / ⑤ The hotel was first

built / in 1932. / ⑥ And / it started / to protect giraffes / in the 1970s. / ⑦

The hotel's goal is / to increase the giraffe population. / (⑧ Healthy giraffes

can live / for 25 years / in the wild. /) ⑨ The hotel is slowly returning the

giraffes / to the wild. / ⑩ Hotel guests can see the giraffes / up close. / ⑪

If they are lucky, / they can also feed them. / ⑫ Giraffes love to eat grass

pellets / at breakfast. / ⑬ Where else can you enjoy breakfast / with a

giraffe? /

1 내 주름에는 비밀이 있어!

① There are many ways / to stay cool / in the animal world. / ②

Kanga-roos lick / their arms. / ③ Dogs stick out / their tongues. / ④ But /

elephants can't do either. / ⑤ They have other special ways / to keep cool.

/ ⑥ One is their wrinkly skin! / ⑦ The wrinkles don't mean / they are old! /

⑧ Even young elephants have them. / (⑨ Elephants can drink / 200 liters

of water / at one time./) ⑩ The wrinkles keep / five to ten times more

water / than smooth skin. / ⑪ That means / it takes longer / for their skin /

to dry out. / ⑫ This is great / for staying cool longer / in hot and dry Africa.

/ ⑬ Elephants in Asia / live in wetter forests, / so they have fewer wrinkles

/ than ones in Africa. /

2 하룻밤 사이에 무슨 일이?!

① A popsicle is a frozen treat / on a stick. / ② Many American kids

enjoy it / in summer. / ③ Do you know / this treat's interesting story? /

④ Actually, / it came from a kid's mistake. /

⑤ It was winter / in 1905. / ⑥ Frank Epperson was 11 years old. / ⑦ He

was making up a drink. / ⑧ He mixed sweet soda powder and water / with

a stick. / ⑨ He left his drink / on the porch / with the stick still in it. / ⑩ He

completely forgot about it. / ⑪ He came back / the next day. / ⑫ The drink

was frozen! / ⑬ But he didn't throw it away. / ⑭ Instead, / he licked it. /

⑮ Wow! / ⑯ It was delicious. / ⑰ The first popsicle was born. /

3 거기 아무도 없나요?

① Most people around the world / have lively New Year's parties. / ②

But / the Balinese welcome their New Year / differently. / ③ They celebrate

it / with Nyepi! /

④ Nyepi is a day / of silence. / ⑤ It takes place / on the first day / of

the Balinese *saka* calendar. / ⑥ It starts / at 6 a.m. / and continues / for 24

hours. / ⑦ On this day, / people clear their minds. / ⑧ They don't make any

noise. / ⑨ This helps / keep the balance / between nature and humans. / ⑩

No planes fly / and no restaurants open. / ⑪ People should stay indoors /

on Nyepi. / ⑫ The Balinese think / demons will be fooled / if all is quiet / on

Nyepi. / ⑬ The demons will think / no one is there / and leave. / ⑭ This will

bring / good luck and peace / to Bali. /

1 아래로 더 아래로

① Let's play a fun game. / ② It's called / Down, Down, Down. / ③

First, / find a partner. / ④ Stand about 10 steps away / from each other. /

⑦ Then / gently throw a tennis ball / back and forth. / ⑥ If no one drops

the ball / for a long time, / each player takes a step back. / ⑤ However, / if

you drop the ball, / you must go down / on one knee. / ⑧ Then / the game

continues. / ⑨ On the second drop, / you must kneel / on both knees. /

⑩ After that, / you have to place one elbow / on the floor / and then put

down the other. / ⑪ The final body part / to go down / is the chin. / ⑫ If

you drop the ball again, / you lose the game. /

2 이 컵이 필요했지?

① In the mid-19th century, / most men grew mustaches. / ② They

wanted / to keep their mustaches neat. / ③ So / they often used wax. /

④ However, / this made enjoying tea difficult. / ⑤ Hot tea could melt

the wax / or get their mustaches wet. / ⑥ It was a big problem / for them.

/ ⑦ Harvey Adams, a British potter, / had an idea. / ⑧ In England during

the 1860s, / he invented / the mustache cup! / ⑨ This special cup had / a

small barrier. / ⑩ It protected the mustache / by covering it. / ⑪ It also had

a small hole / to drink through. /

⑫ Finally / a gentleman could have a handsome mustache / and enjoy

his tea time. / ⑬ Soon / mustache cups became popular / all over Europe. /

3 그림을 다시 보면?

① You might think / Renaissance art is very boring. / ② But / Giuseppe

Arcimboldo's work is fun. / ③ He was an artist / of the 16th century. / ④

He painted / some playful portraits. / ⑤ From a distance, / they look like

people. / ⑥ But / look closely! / ⑦ Those people are made of / various

items / such as food, flowers, and books. /

⑧ An example of his work / is *The Vegetable Gardener*. / ⑨ It is a

painting / of vegetables / in a bowl. / (⑩ You can get healthy vitamins /

from vegetables.) / ⑪ When you turn the painting upside down, / someone

is smiling at you! / ⑫ The onion is a fat cheek, / the large parsnip is a long

nose, / and the mushrooms are lips. / ⑬ Which items would you use / for

your portrait? /

1 코 좀 확인하겠습니다

① Every fingerprint is unique. / ② Each dog's nose print is unique too! /

③ Look at a dog's nose / closely. / ④ You can see lines. / ⑤ They can help

us / find lost dogs. / ⑥ In Canada, / people already use / these patterns / to

identify dogs. /

⑦ Tags and collars / are often used, / but they can be lost or stolen. /

⑧ Some owners also use / microchips. / ⑨ They are put / inside dogs. / ⑩

This can hurt them. / ⑪ Microchips can also break. / ⑫ So, many people

think / nose prints are better. / (⑬ Dogs have more sensitive noses / than

humans. /) ⑭ Dogs' nose prints don't change / as dogs get older. / ⑮ They

can't be removed either! / ⑯ Also it's easy and painless / to collect nose

prints. / ⑰ So, / dog owners, / hurry up / and register them! /

 휘파람을 불면 안 돼!

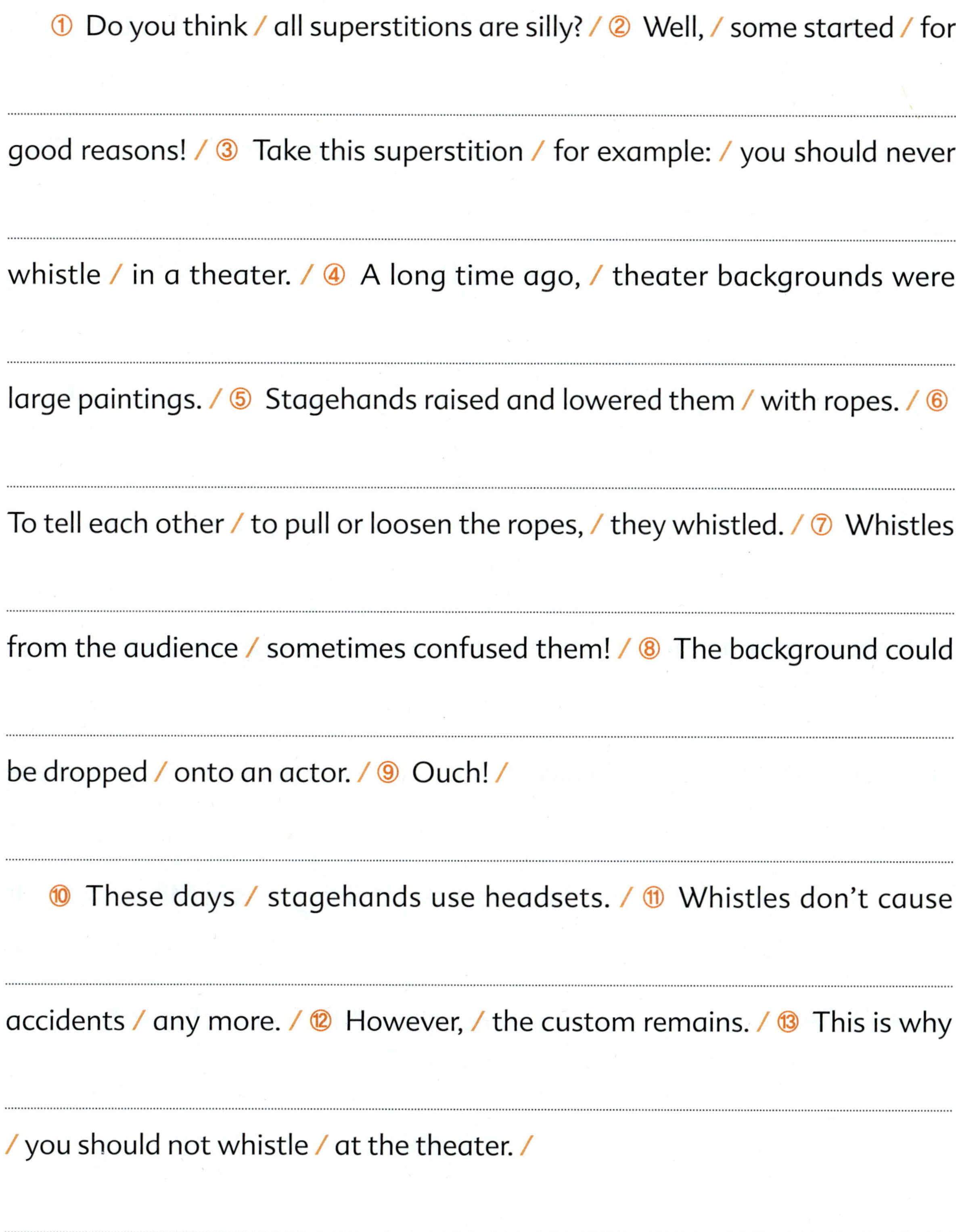

① Do you think / all superstitions are silly? / ② Well, / some started / for good reasons! / ③ Take this superstition / for example: / you should never whistle / in a theater. / ④ A long time ago, / theater backgrounds were large paintings. / ⑤ Stagehands raised and lowered them / with ropes. / ⑥ To tell each other / to pull or loosen the ropes, / they whistled. / ⑦ Whistles from the audience / sometimes confused them! / ⑧ The background could be dropped / onto an actor. / ⑨ Ouch! /

⑩ These days / stagehands use headsets. / ⑪ Whistles don't cause accidents / any more. / ⑫ However, / the custom remains. / ⑬ This is why / you should not whistle / at the theater. /

3 도시는 초록색으로 변화 중!

① Most cities are crowded. / ② There is little space / for trees and

plants / on the ground. / ③ But / cities need plants and trees. / ④ They

clean the air. / ⑤ They also prevent flooding / by absorbing rain. / ⑥

Sometimes, / they provide homes for animals / and help people relax. /

⑦ So / people in cities have found a new place / for plants and trees / —

high above their heads. / ⑧ Architects are now designing buildings / with

outdoor gardens. / ⑨ Hundreds of plants and trees can be grown / in these

gardens. / ⑩ One of the most famous green buildings / is in Milan, Italy. / It

is called / Bosco Verticale. / ⑪ Its name means "the vertical forest." /

1 후~ 생일 축하해

① Cake with candles / is a fun birthday tradition. / ② But / how did it begin? / ③ Cake with candles / dates back / to ancient Greece. / ④ The ancient Greeks / were probably the first / to put candles on cake. / ⑤ They gave gifts / to Artemis, / the goddess of the moon. / ⑥ They gave her / small cakes with candles. / ⑦ The candles made the cakes / glow like the moon. / ⑧ Some people believed / that smoke from candles / carried prayers / to heaven. /

However, / Germans probably made / cake with candles / a birthday tradition. / ⑨ In the 1700s / they started celebrating / children's birthdays / with cake. / ⑩ Parents served a cake / with the same number of candles / as the child's age plus one. / ⑪ It represented / the parents' hope / for their children / to live longer. /

2 앗, 뜨거워!

① In the kitchen, / you burn your hand / on a hot pan. / ② You run / to

get some ice / to ease the pain. / ③ Stop! / ④ Ice doesn't help. /

⑤ Some scientists compared / the treatment effects / of ice and other

cures. / They found / ice actually made the burn / get better more slowly. /

⑥ Also, / ice caused / frostbite and the most serious skin damage. /

⑦ So, / how can we treat a burn? / ⑧ Put the burn / under cool, running

water / for 20 minutes. / ⑨ Or / you can use a cool, wet cloth. / ⑩ Then /

clean the area. / ⑪ In this way, / you can treat most minor burns / at home.

/ ⑫ However, / see a doctor / if your skin doesn't get better / in two weeks. /

3 고래가 나타났다!

① One restorer was cleaning / a 17th-century painting. / ② It was

made / by Dutch painter Hendrick van Anthonissen. / ③ The painting was

a scene / of people on a beach. / ④ But / it had a secret. / ⑤ As she cleaned

the painting, / a thin layer of paint / came off. / ⑥ She saw something

strange. / ⑦ Surprisingly, / it was a huge fin! / ⑧ She continued to remove

/ the layers of paint. / ⑨ Soon / a dead whale appeared / on the beach. /

⑩ But / why was the whale hidden? / ⑪ Researchers said / dead whales

were / an unpleasant subject / for the people of that time. / ⑫ Some

people believed / they meant bad luck. / ⑬ So / it is likely that / the whale

was covered up. / ⑭ But / that's just one guess. / ⑮ We may never know! /

1 앗, 귀가 먹먹해!

① You get on a flight / and put on your seat belt. / ② You want to get

some sleep. / ③ But / sleeping / during takeoff and landing / is not a good

idea. / ④ At these times, / the air pressure in the airplane / changes quickly.

/ ⑤ This changes the pressure / in your ears. / ⑥ Your ears may pop. / ⑦ To

reduce the pressure / in your ears, / you can yawn or swallow. / ⑧ Chewing

gum helps, / too. / ⑨ But / you cannot do these things / when you are

asleep. / ⑩ This could damage your ears. / ⑪ You might feel dizzy. / ⑫ At

worst / you could lose / some of your hearing. / (⑬ Listening to loud music

/ might lead to hearing loss. /)

⑭ So / next time you feel sleepy / on an airplane, / remember: / be

awake / during takeoff and landing. /

① Whistles are useful / for referees. / ② But / they didn't always have them. / ③ At first, / they waved flags and shouted / to get players' attention. / ④ Shouting was fine / for small games. / <u>But / in the 19th century, / sports became popular.</u> / ⑤ The crowds became / bigger and louder. / ⑥ In the noise, / players couldn't hear the referees. / ⑦ Referees really needed something! /

⑧ Inventor Joseph Hudson / gave them a solution. / ⑨ He invented a new whistle / in the 1880s. / ⑩ It was for the police / at first, / but later / he introduced it / to sports. / ⑪ It could be heard / in large crowds. / ⑫ It was much better / than shouting! / ⑬ Soon, / the whistle became common. /

⑭ Now / whistles are used / in most noisy sports, / and even in the Olympics. /

① We feel happy / when we eat delicious food. / ② Gorillas do too, /

and they show it! /

③ Zoologist Eva Luef studied / wild gorillas / in the Congo. / ④ She

found / that they made two different sounds / during meals. / ⑤ One sound

was a deep, steady humming. / ⑥ It sounded / like a sigh of satisfaction. /

⑦ The other sound was like a song. / ⑧ Gorillas sang different notes / to

make their own melody. / ⑨ Each gorilla has / its own style. / ⑩ You can

tell / who is singing. / ⑪ Their songs might tell others / to come and enjoy

the food / with them. / ⑫ When they have their favorite food, / they sing

more loudly! / ⑬ These two habits are ways / to show / their happiness. /

1 일년 내내 메리 크리스마스!

① Do you love Christmas? / ② Then / you'll love Drøbak, Norway. /

③ It's Christmas / all year / in Drøbak! / ④ In Norway, / people say / that

Santa Claus was born / in Drøbak. / ⑤ You can see special street signs /

about Santa / there. / ⑥ They tell you / to watch out for Santa. /

⑦ The village is mainly famous / for Tregaarden's Julehus, or "Christmas

House." / ⑧ You can buy / Christmas decorations and candles / there. / ⑨

Around 250,000 people visit it / each year. / ⑩ And Santa's post office is

next door. / ⑫ You can buy stamps / and send Santa a letter. / ⑪ He will

read your letter / during November and December. / ⑬ If you're lucky, / you

can take a picture / with him / on Christmas Day! /

2 꿀꺽! 껌을 삼켰다고?

① You accidentally swallowed gum. / ② Oops! / ③ According to some people, / now / it will stay / in your body / for seven years. / ④ Is that true? /

⑤ No! / ⑥ Your body treats gum / like any other food. / ⑦ First, / some parts of it / break down / in your stomach. / ⑧ Then / your body saves any nutrients. / ⑨ But / your body cannot digest one part: / the gum base. / ⑩ The chemicals in the gum base / don't break down / easily. / ⑪ So / your body simply pushes it / through your digestive system. / ⑫ And finally / it leaves your body. /

⑬ Swallowing gum / is usually harmless, / but don't make it a habit. /

⑭ Swallowing too much gum / at once / can cause digestive problems! /

3 이래서 블루투스!

① Bluetooth is a wireless technology / to connect devices. / ② This is

used by things / like smartphones, speakers, and earphones! / ③ But / why

is Bluetooth called "Bluetooth"? / ④ Where did the name come from? /

<u>There is an interesting story</u> / behind it. /

⑤ There was a king / in the 10th century. / ⑥ His name was Harald

Gormsson. / ⑦ He was famous / for unifying Denmark and Norway. / ⑧

He loved blueberries so much / that his teeth became blue! / ⑨ So / people

called him / "Bluetooth." /

⑩ The engineers of Bluetooth / named it / after King Harald's

nickname. / ⑪ It connected different devices / like he unified different

lands. /

p. 26

p. 46

p. 66

p. 86

Photo Credits

p. 22   DongDongdog / Shutterstock.com

p. 42   https://commons.wikimedia.org/wiki/File:Portr%C3%A4tt,_Rudolf_II_som_Vertumnus._Guiseppe_
Arcimboldo_-_Skoklosters_slott_-_87582.jpg
https://commons.wikimedia.org/wiki/File:Arcimboldo_Aan_Pot_ful_Gr%C3%A4inieten.jpg

p. 62   https://upload.wikimedia.org/wikipedia/commons/f/fa/Hendrick_van_Anthonissen_-_View_of_Scheveningen_
sands_before_restauration_in_2014.jpg

p. 78   Marcin Kadziolka / Shutterstock.com
Leonard Zhukovsky / Shutterstock.com

others   www.shutterstock.com/
www.istockphoto.com/
https://commons.wikimedia.org/wiki/Main_Page

Reading TUTOR 리딩튜터

Starter 2

어휘 암기장

NE 능률

Section 01

1 크래커도 숨을 쉬어요

popular	형 인기 있는
different	형 다른; 여러 가지의
flavor	명 맛
shape	명 모양
have in common	공통적으로 가지고 있다
hole	명 구멍
important	형 중요한
bubble	명 거품, 기포
dough	명 밀가루 반죽
heat	동 뜨겁게[따뜻하게] 만들다, 가열하다
pop	동 펑 하는 소리가 나다; 펑 하고 터지다
dangerous	형 위험한
strange	형 이상한
machine	명 기계
use	동 사용하다
tiny	형 아주 작은
come out	동 나오다
through	전 ~을 통해
flat	형 평평한
remain	동 계속 ~이다

2 내 빵 돌려내!

fight	동 싸우다(fight-fought-fought) 명 싸움

a piece of	한 조각의
offer	통 제공하다, (기꺼이) 해 주겠다고 하다
split	통 분열되다; 나누다
in half	반으로
agree	통 동의하다
take a bite of	~을 한입 먹다
happen	통 일어나다
again and again	몇 번이고, 되풀이해서
have a full stomach	속이 든든하다, 배부르다
hungry	형 배고픈
clever	형 영리한
trick	명 속임수
share	통 함께 쓰다; 나누다
winner	명 승자
battle	명 전투
soft	형 부드러운
warm	형 따뜻한
equal	형 (수·양·가치 등이) 동일한[같은]

be filled with	~로 가득 차다
smell	명 냄새 통 냄새가 나다
rest	명 나머지
galaxy	명 은하계
scientist	명 과학자
fart	명 방귀 통 방귀를 뀌다
discover	통 발견하다

rotten	형 썩은, 부패한
see a doctor	진찰을 받다, 병원에 가다
though	부 그렇지만, 하지만
survive	동 살아남다, 생존하다
be covered in	~로 덮이다
similar	형 유사한, 비슷한
smelly	형 냄새나는
secret	명 비밀

Section 02

1 보기보다 무시무시해

dangerous	형 위험한
surprise	동 놀라게 하다
mosquito	명 모기
itchy	형 가려운
bite	명 물기; 물린 상처 동 물다(bite-bit-bitten)
carry	동 들고 있다; (병을) 옮기다
disease	명 병
spread	동 펼치다; 퍼지다
deadly	형 생명을 앗아가는, 치명적인
protect	동 보호하다
avoid	동 방지하다, 막다
way	명 방법
long-sleeved	형 긴 소매의

outside	부 밖에
easily	부 쉽게
safe	형 안전한
calm	형 차분한
helpful	형 도움이 되는
harmful	형 해로운

2 이 조그마한 걸 어디에 쓰지?

pocket	명 주머니
vest	명 조끼
fall out	떨어져 나가다
break	동 깨어지다, 부서지다; 고장 나다 (break-broke-broken)
founder	명 창립자, 설립자
come up with	~을 생각해내다, (해답 등을) 찾아내다
bright	형 밝은; 똑똑한, 영리한
place	명 장소
carry	동 나르다; 가지고 다니다
original	형 원래의, 본래의
stay	동 계속 있다, 그대로 남다
remember	동 기억하다
once	부 한 번; (과거) 한때
origin	명 기원, 유래
huge	형 거대한
empty	형 비어 있는, 빈
useful	형 유용한
colorful	형 형형색색의

protected area	보호 구역
be at risk	위험에 처하다
wild	명 야생 (상태)
goal	명 골; 목표
increase	동 증가시키다, 늘리다
population	명 인구; 개체 수
healthy	형 건강한
return	동 돌아오다; 돌려보내다
guest	명 손님; 투숙객
up close	바로 가까이에서
lucky	형 운이 좋은
feed	동 먹이를 주다
grass	명 풀
breakfast	명 아침(밥), 아침 식사
tourist	명 관광객
danger	명 위험

1 내 주름에는 비밀이 있어!

stay	동 머무르다; (상태를) 유지하다, ~인 채로 있다
cool	형 시원한, 서늘한
lick	동 핥다

stick out	~을 내밀다
tongue	명 혀
wrinkly	형 주름이 있는
wrinkle	명 주름
liter	명 리터(부피의 단위)
smooth	형 매끈한, 매끄러운
wet	형 젖은, 습한
forest	명 숲
type	명 유형, 종류
various	형 여러 가지의, 다양한
purpose	명 목적
effort	명 노력

2 하룻밤 사이에 무슨 일이?!

frozen	형 냉동된
treat	명 특별한 것[선물]; 간식
stick	명 막대기
interesting	형 흥미로운
come from	~에서 나오다, 비롯되다
make up	~을 만들다
drink	명 음료
mix	동 섞다
mixed	형 혼합된
soda	명 탄산음료
powder	명 가루
porch	명 (건물 입구에 지붕이 얹혀 있고 흔히 벽이 둘러진) 현관

still	📍아직, 여전히
completely	📍완전히
forget	📍잊다 (forget-forgot-forgotten)
throw away	📍버리다
instead	📍대신에
be born	📍태어나다
invention	📍발명
flavor	📍맛
mistake	📍실수
business	📍사업
overnight	📍밤사이에, 하룻밤 동안

lively	📍활기 넘치는
Balinese	📍발리 사람 📍발리의
welcome	📍맞이하다, 환영하다
celebrate	📍기념하다, 축하하다
take place	개최되다, 일어나다
calendar	📍달력
continue	📍계속되다[하다]
clear	📍깨끗하게 하다
make noise	소리[소음]를 내다
balance	📍균형
nature	📍자연
plane	📍비행기
indoors	실내에서
demon	📍악령, 귀신

fool	동 속이다
quiet	형 조용한
leave	동 떠나다
bring	동 가져다주다
peace	명 평화
horror	명 공포
sadness	명 슬픔
silence	명 고요, 침묵
quietly	부 조용히

Section 04

1 아래로 더 아래로

step	명 걸음
away	부 떨어져
drop	동 떨어뜨리다 명 낙하
knee	명 무릎
kneel	동 무릎 꿇다
player	명 참가자[선수]
gently	부 부드럽게
throw	동 던지다
back and forth	왔다 갔다
continue	동 계속되다
place	동 놓다[두다]
elbow	명 팔꿈치

chin	명 턱
lose	동 잃어버리다; (경기에서) 지다
origin	명 기원, 유래
rule	명 규칙
exercise	동 운동하다
cheating	명 부정행위
ground	명 땅바닥, 지면

2 이 컵이 필요했지?

grow	동 커지다; 기르다(grow-grew-grown)
mustache	명 콧수염
neat	형 정돈된, 단정한, 깔끔한
melt	동 녹이다[녹다]
potter	명 도예가
invent	동 발명하다
barrier	명 장벽, 벽
cover	동 (보호하기 위해) 가리다, 씌우다
hole	명 구덩이, 구멍
gentleman	명 신사, 양반
culture	명 문화
invention	명 발명

3 그림을 다시 보면?

boring	형 지루한
playful	형 장난기 많은; 재미있는, 우스꽝스러운
portrait	명 초상화

from a distance	멀리서, 멀리 떨어져서
look like	~처럼 보이다
be made of	~로 만들어지다
such as	예를 들어, ~와 같은
example	뗑 예, 사례
vegetable	뗑 채소
healthy	뼹 건강한; 건강에 좋은
upside down	거꾸로
fat	뼹 뚱뚱한
cheek	뗑 볼, 뺨
lip	뗑 입술
self-portrait	뗑 자화상
creative	뼹 창조적인, 창의적인
beauty	뗑 아름다움, 미
random	뼹 무작위의

1 코 좀 확인하겠습니다

fingerprint	뗑 지문
unique	뼹 유일무이한, 독특한
lost	뼹 잃어버린
lose	뎅 잃어버리다(lose-lost-lost)
pattern	뗑 양식; 무늬
identify	뎅 (신원을) 확인하다

tag	명 꼬리표
collar	명 (옷의) 깃; (개 등의 목에 거는) 목걸이
steal	동 훔치다, 도둑질하다(steal-stole-stolen)
owner	명 주인
hurt	동 다치게 하다, 아프게 하다
break	동 깨어지다, 부서지다
sensitive	형 세심한; 민감한
remove	동 제거하다
either	부 ~도 그렇다
painless	형 고통 없는, 아프지 않은
collect	동 모으다, 수집하다
register	동 등록하다
walk	동 걷다; 산책시키다
avoid	동 피하다
raise	동 들어 올리다; 기르다

2 휘파람을 불면 안 돼!

superstition	명 미신
silly	형 어리석은, 바보 같은
good	형 좋은; 타당한
reason	명 이유
whistle	동 휘파람을 불다 명 휘파람
theater	명 극장
background	명 배경
lower	동 내리다
rope	명 밧줄, 로프
pull	동 당기다, 잡아당기다

loosen	통 느슨하게 하다
audience	명 청중, 관중
confuse	통 혼란시키다
drop	통 떨어뜨리다
these days	오늘날
cause	통 초래하다, 일으키다
accident	명 사고, 재해
custom	명 관습
matter	통 중요하다
remain	통 계속 ~이다; (없어지지 않고) 남다
disappear	통 사라지다
signal	명 신호

3 도시는 초록색으로 변화 중!

crowded	형 붐비는
space	명 공간
ground	명 땅바닥; 땅
prevent	통 막다
flooding	명 홍수
absorb	통 흡수하다
home	명 집; 서식지
relax	통 휴식을 취하다
architect	명 건축가
design	통 디자인[설계]하다
building	명 건물
outdoor	형 옥외[야외]의
indoor	형 실내의

garden	몡 뜰, 정원
hundreds of	수백의
famous	혱 유명한
vertical	혱 수직의
underground	혱 지하의
urban	혱 도시의

Section 06

| 1 | 후~ 생일 축하해 |

candle	몡 초, 양초
tradition	몡 전통
begin	동 시작되다[하다]
date back to	~까지 거슬러 올라가다
ancient	혱 고대의
Greek	몡 그리스인
probably	분 아마
first	몡 최초의 인물
goddess	몡 여신
glow	동 빛나다
smoke	몡 연기
carry	동 나르다, 전하다
prayer	몡 기도
celebrate	동 기념하다, 축하하다
serve	동 제공하다, 차려 주다

the number of	~의 수
represent	통 대표하다; 나타내다, 표현하다
hope	명 희망

burn	통 타오르다; 데다, 화상을 입다[입히다]
	명 화상, 덴 상처
pan	명 (손잡이가 있는) 냄비, 팬
ease	통 (고통 등을) 덜어 주다
pain	명 통증, 고통
compare A and B	A와 B를 비교하다
treatment	명 치료
treat	통 대하다; 치료하다
effect	명 효과
cure	명 치료법
serious	형 심각한
damage	명 손상, 피해
cloth	명 천, 옷감
clean	통 (깨끗이) 닦다
area	명 지역; 부분
minor	형 작은, 가벼운
get better	낫다, 호전되다
take care of	~을 돌보다, 신경을 쓰다
careful	형 조심하는

Dutch	형 네덜란드의, 네덜란드인의
scene	명 현장; 장면, 광경
beach	명 해변, 바닷가
thin	형 얇은, 가는
layer	명 막, 층, 겹
come off	떼어지다, 떨어지다
strange	형 이상한
surprisingly	부 놀랍게도
huge	형 거대한
fin	명 지느러미
continue	동 계속하다[되다]
remove	동 제거하다, 없애다
dead	형 죽은
whale	명 고래
appear	동 나타나다
hide	동 감추다, 숨기다(hide-hid-hidden)
unpleasant	형 불쾌한
subject	명 주제, 대상
likely	형 가능성 있는, ~할 것 같은
cover up	~을 완전히 덮다[가리다]
guess	명 추측, 짐작
peace	명 평화
victory	명 승리
bad luck	불운

1 앗, 귀가 먹먹해!

flight	명 비행; 항공기
put on	~을 입다, 착용하다
seat belt	명 안전띠
sleep	명 잠, 수면 동 (잠을) 자다
sleepy	형 졸음이 오는
takeoff	명 이륙
landing	명 착륙
pressure	명 압력
airplane	명 비행기
reduce	동 줄이다, 낮추다
yawn	동 하품하다
swallow	동 침을 삼키다
chew	동 (음식을) 씹다
asleep	형 잠이 든
damage	동 손상을 주다
dizzy	형 어지러운
lose	동 잃다, 상실하다
loss	명 상실, 손실
hearing	명 청력, 청각
loud	형 소리가 큰, 시끄러운
lead to	~로 이어지다
awake	형 깨어 있는

whistle	명 호각, 호루라기
useful	형 유용한
referee	명 심판
not always	항상 ~인 것은 아니다
wave	동 흔들다
flag	명 깃발
shout	동 외치다, 소리치다
attention	명 주의, 주목
crowd	명 사람들, 군중
noise	명 소음
noisy	형 시끄러운
inventor	명 발명가
invent	동 발명하다
solution	명 해결책
introduce	동 (사람을) 소개하다; 내놓다, 도입하다
common	형 흔한
stadium	명 경기장
popular	형 인기 있는

3 흥얼흥얼~ 노래의 의미

delicious	형 아주 맛있는
show	동 보여 주다
wild	형 야생의
meal	명 식사
deep	형 깊은; 낮은, 저음의

steady	형 고정적인, 한결같은
humming	명 콧노래
sound like	~처럼 들리다
sigh	명 한숨, 탄식
note	명 메모; 음조, 음
own	형 자신의
tell	동 말하다; 구별하다
favorite	형 매우 좋아하는
loudly	부 큰 소리로
habit	명 습관
feeling	명 느낌; *pl.* 감정
history	명 역사
difference	명 차이, 차이점

Section 08

1 일 년 내내 메리 크리스마스!

be born	태어나다
street	명 거리, 도로
sign	명 기호, 부호; 표지판
watch out for	~에 대해 주의하다
be famous for	~로 유명하다
mainly	부 주로
decoration	명 장식품
candle	명 양초, 초

visit	동 방문하다
post office	명 우체국
stamp	명 우표
lucky	형 운이 좋은
take a picture	사진을 찍다
origin	명 기원
tradition	명 전통

accidentally	부 잘못하여, 뜻하지 않게
swallow	동 삼키다
according to	~에 따르면
stay	동 머무르다, 남다
treat	동 취급하다, 대하다
part	명 부분
break down	분해되다[하다]
stomach	명 위, 복부
save	동 구하다; 저장하다
nutrient	명 영양소, 영양분
digest	동 소화시키다
digestive	형 소화의
chemical	명 화학 물질
simply	부 그저, 단순히
push	동 밀다, 밀어내다
leave	동 떠나다
harmless	형 해가 없는, 무해한
at once	한꺼번에

wireless	형 무선의
technology	명 (과학) 기술
connect	동 연결하다
device	명 장치, 기기
come from	~에서 나오다, 비롯되다
unify	동 통합하다
engineer	명 엔지니어, 기술자
name after	~의 이름을 따서 명명하다
nickname	명 별명
land	명 땅

Word Review

다음 우리말은 영어로, 영어는 우리말로 쓰시오.

1 popular ___________________

2 flavor ___________________

3 heat ___________________

4 come out ___________________

5 be filled with ___________________

6 fart ___________________

7 rotten ___________________

8 though ___________________

9 similar ___________________

10 split ___________________

11 agree ___________________

12 clever ___________________

13 trick ___________________

14 (수·양·가치 등이) 동일한[같은] ___________________

15 공통적으로 가지고 있다 ___________________

16 위험한 ___________________

17 기계 ___________________

18 계속 ~이다 ___________________

19 냄새; 냄새가 나다 ___________________

20 과학자 ___________________

21 살아남다, 생존하다 ___________________

22 비밀 ___________________

23 싸우다; 싸움 ___________________

24 한 조각의 ___________________

25 함께 쓰다; 나누다 ___________________

다음 우리말은 영어로, 영어는 우리말로 쓰시오.

1 surprise ___________________

2 itchy ___________________

3 protect ___________________

4 harmful ___________________

5 fall out ___________________

6 break ___________________

7 remember ___________________

8 origin ___________________

9 useful ___________________

10 be at risk ___________________

11 population ___________________

12 up close ___________________

13 tourist ___________________

14 모기 ___________________

15 펼치다; 퍼지다 ___________________

16 쉽게 ___________________

17 차분한 ___________________

18 원래의, 본래의 ___________________

19 창립자, 설립자 ___________________

20 ~을 생각해내다, (해답 등을) 찾아내다 ___________________

21 거대한 ___________________

22 야생 (상태) ___________________

23 증가시키다, 늘리다 ___________________

24 돌아오다; 돌려보내다 ___________________

25 운이 좋은 ___________________

다음 우리말은 영어로, 영어는 우리말로 쓰시오.

1 lick __________

2 wrinkly __________

3 smooth __________

4 forest __________

5 frozen __________

6 come from __________

7 still __________

8 throw away __________

9 welcome __________

10 continue __________

11 make noise __________

12 peace __________

13 silence __________

14 ~을 내밀다 __________

15 여러 가지의, 다양한 __________

16 목적 __________

17 노력 __________

18 특별한 것[선물]; 간식 __________

19 흥미로운 __________

20 섞다 __________

21 완전히 __________

22 활기 넘치는 __________

23 개최되다, 일어나다 __________

24 실내에서 __________

25 떠나다 __________

다음 우리말은 영어로, 영어는 우리말로 쓰시오.

1   gently

2   elbow

3   invent

4   melt

5   neat

6   throw

7   back and forth

8   cheating

9   playful

10   healthy

11   example

12   grow

13   creative

14   아름다움, 미

15   문화

16   걸음

17   운동하다

18   무릎

19   떨어져

20   턱

21   규칙

22   초상화

23   무작위의

24   (보호하기 위해) 가리다, 씌우다

25   장벽, 벽

다음 우리말은 영어로, 영어는 우리말로 쓰시오.

1   relax　　　　　　　　　　　_______________________

2   vertical　　　　　　　　　_______________________

3   absorb　　　　　　　　　_______________________

4   accident　　　　　　　　_______________________

5   silly　　　　　　　　　　_______________________

6   superstition　　　　　　　_______________________

7   identify　　　　　　　　　_______________________

8   tag　　　　　　　　　　　_______________________

9   confuse　　　　　　　　　_______________________

10   audience　　　　　　　　_______________________

11   either　　　　　　　　　_______________________

12   attention　　　　　　　　_______________________

13   pattern　　　　　　　　　_______________________

14   등록하다　　　　　　　　_______________________

15   지문　　　　　　　　　　_______________________

16   사라지다　　　　　　　　_______________________

17   들어 올리다; 기르다　　　_______________________

18   이유　　　　　　　　　　_______________________

19   건축가　　　　　　　　　_______________________

20   주인　　　　　　　　　　_______________________

21   당기다, 잡아당기다　　　_______________________

22   극장　　　　　　　　　　_______________________

23   계속 ~이다; (없어지지 않고) 남다　_______________________

24   땅바닥; 땅　　　　　　　_______________________

25   붐비는　　　　　　　　　_______________________

다음 우리말은 영어로, 영어는 우리말로 쓰시오.

1 peace ___________________

2 hide ___________________

3 huge ___________________

4 strange ___________________

5 minor ___________________

6 serious ___________________

7 pain ___________________

8 glow ___________________

9 treatment ___________________

10 ease ___________________

11 compare A and B ___________________

12 area ___________________

13 ancient ___________________

14 불쾌한 ___________________

15 불운 ___________________

16 승리 ___________________

17 초, 양초 ___________________

18 제공하다, 차려 주다 ___________________

19 대하다; 치료하다 ___________________

20 효과 ___________________

21 현장; 장면, 광경 ___________________

22 기도 ___________________

23 추측, 짐작 ___________________

24 고래 ___________________

25 연기 ___________________

다음 우리말은 영어로, 영어는 우리말로 쓰시오.

1 habit _______________

2 history _______________

3 meal _______________

4 common _______________

5 reduce _______________

6 pressure _______________

7 useful _______________

8 loud _______________

9 lead to _______________

10 put on _______________

11 lose _______________

12 attention _______________

13 delicious _______________

14 고정적인, 한결같은 _______________

15 보여 주다 _______________

16 비행; 항공기 _______________

17 (음식을) 씹다 _______________

18 외치다, 소리치다 _______________

19 소음 _______________

20 인기 있는 _______________

21 말하다; 구별하다 _______________

22 한숨, 탄식 _______________

23 손상을 주다 _______________

24 어지러운 _______________

25 깨어 있는 _______________

다음 우리말은 영어로, 영어는 우리말로 쓰시오.

1 harmless ____________________

2 digest ____________________

3 nickname ____________________

4 street ____________________

5 visit ____________________

6 swallow ____________________

7 part ____________________

8 save ____________________

9 chemical ____________________

10 device ____________________

11 unify ____________________

12 lucky ____________________

13 be born ____________________

14 전통 ____________________

15 영양소, 영양분 ____________________

16 (과학) 기술 ____________________

17 머무르다, 남다 ____________________

18 잘못하여, 뜻하지 않게 ____________________

19 밀다, 밀어내다 ____________________

20 떠나다 ____________________

21 연결하다 ____________________

22 장식품 ____________________

23 기원 ____________________

24 ~에 따르면 ____________________

25 ~의 이름을 따서 명명하다 ____________________

Word Review 정답

Section 01

1 인기 있는 2 맛 3 뜨겁게[따뜻하게] 만들다, 가열하다 4 나오다 5 ~로 가득 차다 6 방귀; 방귀를 뀌다 7 썩은, 부패한 8 그렇지만, 하지만 9 유사한, 비슷한 10 분열되다; 나누다 11 동의하다 12 영리한 13 속임수 14 equal 15 have in common 16 dangerous 17 machine 18 remain 19 smell 20 scientist 21 survive 22 secret 23 fight 24 a piece of 25 share

Section 02

1 놀라게 하다 2 가려운 3 보호하다 4 해로운 5 떨어져 나가다 6 깨어지다, 부서지다; 고장 나다 7 기억하다 8 기원, 유래 9 유용한 10 위험에 처하다 11 인구; 개체 수 12 바로 가까이에서 13 관광객 14 mosquito 15 spread 16 easily 17 calm 18 original 19 founder 20 come up with 21 huge 22 wild 23 increase 24 return 25 lucky

Section 03

1 핥다 2 주름이 있는 3 매끈한, 매끄러운 4 숲 5 냉동된 6 ~에서 나오다, 비롯되다 7 아직, 여전히 8 버리다 9 맞이하다, 환영하다 10 계속되다[하다] 11 소리[소음]를 내다 12 평화 13 고요, 침묵 14 stick out 15 various 16 purpose 17 effort 18 treat 19 interesting 20 mix 21 completely 22 lively 23 take place 24 indoors 25 leave

Section 04

1 부드럽게 2 팔꿈치 3 발명하다 4 녹이다[녹다] 5 정돈된, 단정한, 깔끔한 6 던지다 7 왔다 갔다 8 부정행위 9 장난기 많은; 재미있는, 우스꽝스러운 10 건강한; 건강에 좋은 11 예, 사례 12 커지다; 기르다 13 창조적인, 창의적인 14 beauty 15 culture 16 step 17 exercise 18 knee 19 away 20 chin 21 rule 22 portrait 23 random 24 cover 25 barrier

Section 05

1 휴식을 취하다 2 수직의 3 흡수하다 4 사고, 재해 5 어리석은, 바보 같은 6 미신 7 (신원을) 확인하다 8 꼬리표 9 혼란시키다 10 청중, 관중 11 ~도 그렇다 12 주의, 주목 13 양식; 무늬 14 register 15 fingerprint 16 disappear 17 raise 18 reason 19 architect 20 owner 21 pull 22 theater 23 remain 24 ground 25 crowded

Section 06

1 평화 2 감추다, 숨기다 3 거대한 4 이상한 5 작은, 가벼운 6 심각한 7 통증, 고통 8 빛나다 9 치료 10 (고통 등을) 덜어 주다 11 A와 B를 비교하다 12 지역; 부분 13 고대의 14 unpleasant 15 bad luck 16 victory 17 candle 18 serve 19 treat 20 effect 21 scene 22 prayer 23 guess 24 whale 25 smoke

Section 07

1 습관 2 역사 3 식사 4 흔한 5 줄이다, 낮추다 6 압력 7 유용한 8 소리가 큰, 시끄러운 9 ~로 이어지다 10 ~을 입다, 착용하다 11 잃다, 상실하다 12 주의, 주목 13 아주 맛있는 14 steady 15 show 16 flight 17 chew 18 shout 19 noise 20 popular 21 tell 22 sigh 23 damage 24 dizzy 25 awake

Section 08

1 해가 없는, 무해한 2 소화시키다 3 별명 4 거리, 도로 5 방문하다 6 삼키다 7 부분 8 구하다; 저장하다 9 화학 물질 10 장치, 기기 11 통합하다 12 운이 좋은 13 태어나다 14 tradition 15 nutrient 16 technology 17 stay 18 accidentally 19 push 20 leave 21 connect 22 decoration 23 origin 24 according to 25 name after

MEMO

BOOK LIST

도/서/목/록

초등 초등영어 된다 시리즈

초등영어 리딩이 된다

교과 내용을 영어로 쉽고 재미있게
학습하는 초등 독해서
START   1 | 2 | 3 | 4
BASIC   1 | 2 | 3 | 4
JUMP   1 | 2 | 3 | 4

초등영어 문법이 된다

초등 교육과정을 기반으로 한 영문법 학습서
Starter 1 | Starter 2 | 1 | 2

초등영어 단어가 된다

교육부 권장 초등 필수 영단어 학습서
1 | 2 | 3 | 4

초등영어 파닉스가 된다

알파벳 음가 블랜딩 연습을 통해
읽기 유창성을 기르는 파닉스 학습서
1 | 2

초등영어 사이트 워드가 된다

영어 읽기 독립을 위한 사이트 워드 학습서
1 | 2

독해

Reading TUTOR 리딩튜터

체계적인 초·중·고등 독해 프로그램
Starter   1 | 2 | 3
Junior   1 | 2 | 3 | 4
리딩튜터   입문 | 기본 | 실력 | 수능PLUS

달곰한 LITERACY (Reading)

초등학생을 위한 문해력 기본서
LEVEL   1 | 2 | 3
LEVEL   4 | 5 | 6

READING BUDDY

초등학생을 위한 독해 입문서
1 | 2 | 3
Grammar Buddy | Listening Buddy

어휘

주니어 능률 VOCA

대한민국 중등 어휘 교재의 표준
Starter 1 | Starter 2 |
입문 | 기본 | 실력 | 숙어

해당 교재와 연계되는 시리즈

Reading TUTOR 리딩 튜터

Starter 2

정답 및 해설

NE 능률

Reading TUTOR 리딩튜터

Starter 2

정답 및 해설

SECTION 01

정답 1 ② 2 ④ 3 ⑤ 4 flat[perfect], perfect[flat]

문제 해설

1 크래커를 만들 때 크래커의 평평한 모양을 유지하기 위해 반죽에 구멍을 만들게 되었다는 내용의 글이므로, 주제로는 ②가 가장 알맞다.

2 크래커에 구멍을 만든 이유를 설명하는 내용 중에, 뜨거운 오븐은 위험할 수 있다는 내용의 (d)는 흐름상 어색하다.

3 문장 ⑬-⑭를 통해 알 수 있다.

4 문장 ⑭-⑮에 언급되어 있다.

> 크래커는 그 안의 구멍들 때문에 모양이 <u>평평하고 완벽하게</u> 유지된다.

본문 직독 직해

① Crackers are a popular snack. / ② They have different flavors. / ③ There are many
크래커는 인기 있는 간식이다   그것들은 여러 가지 맛이 있다   많은

shapes and sizes, too. / ④ But / they have one thing in common. / ⑤ They all have
모양과 크기도 있다   하지만 그것들은 한 가지를 공통적으로 가지고 있다   그것들은 모두 구멍들을

holes. / ⑥ The holes are important. / ⑦ There are air bubbles / in cracker dough. / ⑧ The
가지고 있다   그 구멍들은 중요하다   기포가 있다   크래커 반죽에는

dough is heated / in an oven. / ⑨ Then the bubbles get bigger / and pop. / (⑩ Hot
반죽이 가열된다   오븐에서   그러면 기포는 더 커진다   그리고 터진다   뜨거운

ovens can be dangerous. /) ⑪ This gives crackers a strange shape. / ⑫ So / a special
오븐은 위험할 수 있다   이것은 크래커를 이상한 모양으로 만든다   그래서 한 특별한

machine is used. / ⑬ It makes tiny holes / in the crackers. / ⑭ The air comes out /
기계가 사용된다   그것은 아주 작은 구멍들을 만든다   크래커에   공기는 나온다

through the holes. / ⑮ Finally, / the crackers stay flat / and perfect! /
그 구멍들을 통해   마침내   크래커는 평평하게 유지된다   그리고 완벽하게

본문 해석

크래커는 인기 있는 간식이다. 그것들은 여러 가지 맛이 있다. 많은 모양과 크기도 있다. 하지만 그것들은 한 가지를 공통적으로 가지고 있다. 그것들은 모두 구멍들을 가지고 있다. 그 구멍들은 중요하다. 크래커 반죽에는 기포가 있다. 반죽이 오븐에서 가열된다. 그러면 기포는 더 커지며 터진다. (뜨거운 오븐은 위험할 수 있다.) 이것은 크래커를 이상한 모양으로 만든다. 그래서 한 특별한 기계가 사용된다. 그것은 크래커에 아주 작은 구멍들을 만든다. 공기는 그 구멍들을 통해 나온다. 마침내 크래커는 평평하고 완벽하게 유지된다!

구문 해설

⑧ The dough **is heated** in an oven.
→ is heated는 '가열되다'의 의미로, 「be+p.p.」의 수동태이다.

⑨ Then the bubbles ***get bigger*** and *pop*.
→ 「get+형용사의 비교급」은 '더 ~해지다'의 의미이다.
→ 문장의 동사 get과 pop이 접속사 and로 병렬 연결되어 있다.

정답   **1** ①   **2** ③   **3** (1) T (2) F   **4** ②

문제 해설

1 두 고양이가 빵 한 조각을 두고 싸우는 것을 본 원숭이가 꾀를 내어 빵을 다 먹어버렸다는 내용이므로, 제목으로는 ① '영리한 원숭이의 속임수'가 가장 알맞다.

② 음식을 나누는 방법　　　　　　　③ 큰 싸움의 승자

④ 고양이들이 빵을 좋아하지 않는 이유　　　⑤ 고양이와 원숭이의 전투

2 빈칸 앞에는 빵을 반으로 나누었는데 한쪽이 더 크다는 내용이 나오고, 빈칸 뒤에는 원숭이가 더 큰 빵을 한입 먹었다는 내용이 나오므로, 빈칸에는 ③ '동일한'이 가장 알맞다.

① 부드러운 ② 따뜻한 ④ 특별한 ⑤ 다른

3 (1) 문장 ①에 언급되어 있다.

(2) 문장 ⑮에서 두 고양이는 배가 고픈 채로 집으로 돌아갔다고 했다.

4 원숭이가 고양이들의 빵을 다 먹어버렸으므로, 두 고양이의 심경으로는 ②가 알맞다.

본문 직독 직해

① Two cats fought for a piece of bread. / ② They both wanted it. / ③ A smart monkey
두 고양이가 빵 한 조각을 놓고 싸웠다　　　　그들은 둘 다 그것을 원했다　　　똑똑한 원숭이가

saw them / and offered to help. / ④ He said / he'd split the bread / in half. / ⑤ The cats
그들을 봤다　　그리고 도와주겠다고 했다　　그는 말했다　그가 빵을 나누겠다고　　반으로　　고양이들은

agreed. / ⑥ The monkey split the bread / in half. / ⑦ One piece was bigger / than the
동의했다　　　원숭이가 빵을 나눴다　　　　반으로　　　한 조각이 더 컸다　　　다른 것보다

other. / ⑧ The monkey wanted them / to be equal. / ⑨ He took a bite / of the bigger
원숭이는 그것들을 원했다　　　동일하기를　　　그는 한입 베어 물었다　더 큰 조각을

piece. / ⑩ Now / the other piece was bigger. / ⑪ This happened / again and again. /
이제　　다른 조각이 더 컸다　　　　　이런 일이 있었다　　몇 번이고

⑫ Soon / the bread was gone. / ⑬ The monkey had a full stomach. / ⑭ The cats
곧　　　그 빵은 사라졌다　　　　원숭이는 배가 불렀다　　　　　고양이들은

didn't get anything. / ⑮ They went home hungry. /
아무것도 얻지 못했다　　　그들은 배가 고픈 채로 집으로 돌아갔다

본문 해석

　　두 고양이가 빵 한 조각을 놓고 싸웠다. 그들은 둘 다 그것을 원했다. 똑똑한 원숭이가 그들을 보고 도와주겠다고 했다. 그는 빵을 반으로 나누겠다고 말했다. 고양이들은 동의했다. 원숭이가 빵을 반으로 나눴다. 한 조각이 다른 조각보다 더 컸다. 원숭이는 그것들이 <u>동일하기를</u> 원했다. 그는 더 큰 조각을 한입 베어 물었다. 이제 다른 조각이 더 컸다. 이런 일이 몇 번이고 있었다. 곧 그 빵은 사라졌다. 원숭이는 배가 불렀다. 고양이들은 아무것도 얻지 못했다. 그들은 배가 고픈 채로 집으로 돌아갔다.

① Two cats fought for **a piece of bread**.

➜ 셀 수 없는 명사 bread는 수량을 표현하고 싶을 때, '조각'의 의미로 a piece of를 쓴다.

④ He said [**(that)** he'*d* split the bread in half].

➜ [ ]는 동사 said의 목적어 역할을 하는 명사절로, 접속사 that이 생략되었다.

➜ 'd는 조동사 would의 줄임말로, '~할 것이다'의 의미인 will이 주절의 과거시제에 맞춰 과거형으로 쓰였다.

⑦ **One piece** was *bigger than* **the other**.

➜ 대상이 두 가지로 정해져 있을 때 둘 중 하나는 one으로, 다른 하나는 the other로 나타낸다.

➜ 「형용사의 비교급+than」은 '~보다 더 …한'의 의미이다.

⑧ The monkey **wanted them to be** equal.

➜ 「want+목적어+to-v」는 '~가 …하기를 원하다'의 의미이다.

⑮ They went home **hungry**.

➜ 형용사 hungry는 동사 went와 함께 쓰여 주어(They)의 상태를 설명하는 서술용법으로 쓰였다.

본책 • pp. 12-13

정답   1 ②   2 ⑤   3 ④   4 (그곳이 약 영하 200도라서) 인간이 (1초도) 생존할 수 없기 때문에

**문제
해설**

1 천왕성에서 방귀 냄새가 나는 이유를 설명하는 글이므로, 제목으로는 ② '천왕성의 냄새 나는 비밀'이 가장 알맞다.

① 은하계를 여행하는 방법   ③ 인간은 천왕성에서 생존할 수 있는가?

④ 우리는 은하계에서 무엇이든 냄새를 맡을 수 있는가?   ⑤ 천왕성: 은하계에서 가장 추운 행성

2 천왕성의 방귀 냄새에 대한 연구를 설명하는 내용 중에, 방귀를 자주 뀌면 진찰을 받아야 한다는 내용의 (e)는 글의 흐름과 무관하다.

3 ④: 천왕성을 최초로 발견한 사람은 언급되지 않았다.

①은 문장 ⑦, ②는 문장 ⑧, ③은 문장 ⑫, 그리고 ⑤는 문장 ⑮를 통해 알 수 있다.

4 문장 ⑫–⑬에 언급되어 있다.

**본문
직독
직해**

① The world is filled / with many different smells. / ② But / what does the rest
세상은 가득 차 있다　　다양한 냄새로　　　　　　그런데　은하계의 나머지는

of the galaxy smell like? / ③ Well, / scientists can tell you / about one planet. / ④ Uranus
어떤 냄새가 날까　　　자　과학자들은 당신에게 알려줄 수 있다　한 행성에 대해　　천왕성은

smells like farts! / ⑤ How do they know? / ⑥ They studied / the clouds of Uranus. /
방귀 냄새가 난다　　그들이 어떻게 알까　　그들은 연구했다　천왕성의 구름을

⑦ They discovered / the clouds are made of / hydrogen sulfide. / ⑧ This gas smells /
그들은 발견했다　　그 구름이 ~로 이루어져 있다는 것을　황화수소로　　　이 가스는 냄새가 난다

like farts or rotten eggs. / (⑨ If you fart too often, / you should see a doctor.) ⑩ Don't
방귀나 썩은 달걀 같은　　　　당신이 너무 자주 방귀를 뀐다면　당신은 진찰을 받아야 한다　　걱정하지

worry / though. / ⑪ You will never smell Uranus. / ⑫ It's about -200°C there!
마라　하지만　　당신이 천왕성 냄새를 맡을 일은 결코 없을 것이다　그곳은 약 영하 200도이다

⑬ Humans can't survive / even for a second! /
인간은 생존할 수 없다　　1초도

⑭ Now / scientists are looking at Neptune. / ⑮ They think / it might be covered / in a
이제　　과학자들은 해왕성을 살피고 있다　　　　　　　　그들은 생각한다　그것이 덮여 있을지도 모른다고

similar gas. /
비슷한 기체로

본문 해석

　　세상은 다양한 냄새로 가득 차 있다. 그런데 은하계의 나머지는 어떤 냄새가 날까? 자, 과학자들은 한 행성에 대해서는 알려줄 수 있다. 천왕성은 방귀 냄새가 난다! 그들이 어떻게 알까? 그들은 천왕성의 구름을 연구했다. 그들은 그 구름이 황화수소로 이루어져 있다는 것을 발견했다. 이 가스는 방귀나 썩은 달걀 같은 냄새가 난다. (당신이 너무 자주 방귀를 뀐다면, 진찰을 받아야 한다.) 하지만 걱정하지 마라. 당신이 천왕성 냄새를 맡을 일은 결코 없을 것이다. 그곳은 약 영하 200도이다! 인간은 1초도 생존할 수 없다!

　　이제 과학자들은 해왕성을 살피고 있다. 그들은 그것이 비슷한 기체로 덮여 있을지도 모른다고 생각한다.

구문 해설

④ Uranus **smells like** farts!
→ 「smell like ~」는 '~의 냄새가 나다'의 의미로, 뒤에 명사가 온다.

⑦ They discovered [**(that)** the clouds are made of hydrogen sulfide].
→ [ ]는 동사 discovered의 목적어 역할을 하는 명사절로, 접속사 that이 생략되었다.

⑭ Now scientists **are looking** at Neptune.
→ are looking은 '살피고 있다'의 의미로, 「be동사의 현재형＋v-ing」의 현재진행형이다.

⑮ They think [**(that)** it might be covered in a similar gas].
→ [ ]는 동사 think의 목적어 역할을 하는 명사절로, 접속사 that이 생략되었다.

정답

1 split **2** dough **3** fight **4** smell **5** scientist **6** bubble **7** ⓒ **8** ⓐ
9 ⓑ **10** ③ **11** ⑤ **12** take a bite of **13** see a doctor **14** have in common
15 the bubbles get bigger and pop
16 The world is filled with many different smells.
17 One piece was bigger than the other.

문제 해설

1 split: 나누다

2 dough: 밀가루 반죽

3 fight: 싸우다

4 smell: 냄새가 나다

5 scientist: 과학자

6 bubble: 거품, 기포

7 trick(속임수): ⓒ 누군가를 속이는 영리한 방법

8 heat(가열하다): ⓐ 어떤 것을 따뜻하거나 뜨겁게 만들다

9 discover(발견하다): ⓑ 알려지지 않은 것을 찾아내다

10 그 쿠키는 부드럽고 달콤했다.

① 평평한 ② 따뜻한 ③ 딱딱한 ④ 인기 있는 ⑤ 중요한

11 이 두 셔츠는 색깔이 매우 비슷해 보인다.

① 동일한 ② 이상한 ③ 작은 ④ 썩은 ⑤ 다른

12 take a bite of: ~을 한입 먹다

13 see a doctor: 진찰을 받다, 병원에 가다

14 have in common: 공통적으로 가지고 있다

15 '더 ~해지다'라는 의미의 「get+형용사의 비교급」을 쓴다.

16 '~로 가득 차다'라는 의미의 be filled with를 쓴다.

17 '(둘 중) 하나는 ~, 다른 하나는 …'이라는 의미의 「one ~, the other …」를 쓴다. '~보다 더 …한'이라는 의미의 「형용사의 비교급+than」을 쓴다.

SECTION 02

1

정답 **1** ④ **2** (1) T (2) F **3** ① **4** dangerous, diseases

문제 해설

1 모기가 사람을 물 때 생명에 치명적인 질병을 옮길 수 있어서 세상에서 가장 위험한 동물이라는 내용의 글이므로, 주제로는 ④가 가장 알맞다.

2 (1) 문장 ⑨-⑪에 언급되어 있다.

(2) 문장 ⑭에서 모기에 물리지 않기 위한 방법으로 소매가 긴 셔츠를 입으라고 했다.

3 빈칸 앞에서 모기에게 물리지 않는 방법으로 소매가 긴 셔츠와 긴 바지를 입으라고 제안하고 있으므로, 빈칸에는 ① '더 안전한'이 가장 알맞다.

② 더 긴 ③ 더 차분한 ④ 덜 도움이 되는 ⑤ 더 해로운

4 모기는 치명적인 질병들을 옮길 수 있기 때문에 가장 위험하다.

본문 직독 직해

① Think of / the world's most dangerous animal. / ② Are they snakes? / ③ Sharks?
생각해 보아라 세상에서 가장 위험한 동물을   그것들은 뱀일까   상어

Bears? / ④ The answer may surprise you. / ⑤ It is mosquitoes. /
곰   그 대답이 당신을 놀라게 할지도 모른다   그것은 모기이다

⑥ Why are mosquitoes so dangerous? / ⑦ You might not worry / about an itchy
왜 모기들은 그렇게 위험할까   당신은 걱정하지 않을지도 모른다   가려운

mosquito bite. / ⑧ But / it can become a big problem. / ⑨ Many mosquitoes carry
모기 물린 곳에 대해   그러나 그것은 큰 문제가 될 수 있다.   많은 모기들이 질병들을 옮긴다

diseases. / ⑩ These diseases can spread / when they bite humans. / ⑪ Such diseases
                이 질병들은 퍼질 수 있다   그것들이 사람을 물 때   이러한 질병들은

can be deadly. /
치명적일 수 있다

⑫ So, / how can you protect yourself / from mosquitoes? / ⑬ Avoiding mosquito
그렇다면 당신은 어떻게 스스로를 보호할 수 있을까   모기들로부터   모기에 물리지 않는 것이

bites is the best way. / ⑭ Wear a long-sleeved shirt / outside. / ⑮ Wear long pants, too. /
가장 좋은 방법이다   긴 소매 셔츠를 입어라   밖에서   긴 바지를 입어라   또한

⑯ Then / mosquitoes cannot bite you / easily. / ⑰ It may be hotter, / but it is safer! /
그러면   모기는 당신을 물 수 없다   쉽게   더 더울지 모르지만   더 안전하다

본문 해석

세상에서 가장 위험한 동물을 생각해 보아라. 그것들은 뱀일까? 상어? 곰? 그 대답이 당신을 놀라게 할지도 모른다. 그것은 모기이다.

왜 모기들은 그렇게 위험할까? 당신은 가려운 모기 물린 곳에 대해 걱정하지 않을지도 모른다. 그러나 그것은 큰 문제가 될 수 있다. 많은 모기들이 질병들을 옮긴다. 이 질병들은 그것들이 사람을 물 때 퍼질 수 있다. 이러한 질병들은 치명적일 수 있다.

그렇다면, 당신은 어떻게 모기들로부터 스스로를 보호할 수 있을까? 모기에 물리지 않는 것이 가장 좋은 방법이다. 밖에서 긴 소매 셔츠를 입어라. 긴 바지도 입어라. 그러면 모기는 당신을 쉽게 물 수 없다. 더 더울지 모르지만, 더 안전하다!

① **Think** of the world's *most dangerous* animal.
  → 동사원형 Think가 문장 맨 앞에 와서 명령문으로 쓰였다.
  → 3음절 이상의 형용사 dangerous의 최상급은 most dangerous로 쓴다.
⑫ So, how can you protect **yourself** from mosquitoes?
  → 동사 protect의 목적어가 주어(you)와 같은 대상을 가리키므로 재귀대명사가 쓰였다.
⑬ [*Avoiding* mosquito bites] *is* the best way.
  → [ ]는 주어 역할을 하는 동명사구이다.
  → 동명사(구)는 단수 취급하므로 단수형 동사 is가 쓰였다.

본책 • pp. 20–21

정답 **1** ② **2** ④ **3** pocket watches **4** 청바지 회사가 본래의 디자인을 유지하길 원하기 때문에

문제 해설

1 과거에 청바지의 작은 주머니가 회중시계를 넣는 용도를 위해 만들어졌다는 내용의 글이므로, 제목으로는 ② '청바지에 있는 작은 주머니의 유래'가 가장 알맞다.
  ① 최고의 회중시계 고르기　　　　　　　　　③ 1800년대 일꾼들은 무엇을 입었는가?
  ④ 누가 주머니가 있는 최초의 청바지를 만들었는가?　　⑤ 세계 최초의 청바지 회사

2 과거에는 일꾼들이 회중시계를 청바지 주머니에 보관했다고 했으므로, 빈칸에는 ④ '유용한'이 가장 알맞다.
  ① 거대한　② 비어 있는　③ 독특한　⑤ 형형색색의

3 문장 ⑦-⑧에 언급되어 있다.

> 청바지에 있는 아주 작은 주머니는 일꾼들의 회중시계를 위해 디자인되었다.

4 문장 ⑩-⑪에 언급되어 있다.

본문 직독 직해

① Have you seen strange, tiny pockets / on your jeans? / ② You cannot put much / in
이상하고 아주 작은 주머니를 본 적이 있는가　청바지에 있는　당신은 많은 것을 넣을 수 없다
them. / ③ So, / what are they for? / ④ Well, / back in the late 1800s, / people had pocket
그것들 안에　그렇다면 그것들은 무엇을 위한 것인가　그러니까 과거 1800년대 후반에　사람들은 회중시계를
watches! / ⑤ Workers usually put their watches / in their vests. / ⑥ But / their watches
가지고 다녔다　일꾼들은 보통 그들의 시계를 넣었다　조끼 안에　하지만 그들의 시계가
often fell out / and broke. /
자주 떨어졌다　그리고 고장 났다
⑦ Denim jeans company founder Levi Strauss / came up with a bright idea: / a watch
청바지 회사 창립자인 리바이 스트라우스가　기발한 아이디어를 생각해 냈다　시계
pocket! / ⑧ Workers could finally keep their watches / in a safe place. / ⑨ Today / few
주머니다　일꾼들은 마침내 그들의 시계를 보관할 수 있었다　안전한 곳에　오늘날　가지고
people carry / pocket watches. / ⑩ However, / the company wants / to keep the original
다니는 사람은 거의 없다 회중시계를　하지만　그 회사는 원한다　본래의 디자인을 유지하기를
design. / ⑪ So / the pockets have stayed. / ⑫ The next time you see / that little pocket, /
그래서 주머니가 그대로 남았다　다음에 당신이 보면　그 작은 주머니를
remember / it was once useful! /
기억하라　그것이 한때는 유용했다는 것을

청바지에 있는 이상하고 아주 작은 주머니를 본 적이 있는가? 그것들 안에 많은 것을 넣을 수 없다. 그렇다면, 그것들은 무엇을 위한 것인가? 그러니까, 과거 1800년대 후반에, 사람들은 회중시계를 가지고 다녔다! 일꾼들은 보통 조끼 안에 시계를 넣었다. 하지만 시계가 자주 떨어져서 고장 났다.

청바지 회사 창립자인 리바이 스트라우스가 기발한 아이디어를 생각해 냈는데, 바로 시계 주머니다! 일꾼들은 마침내 그들의 시계를 안전한 곳에 보관할 수 있었다. 오늘날 회중시계를 가지고 다니는 사람은 거의 없다. 하지만 그 회사는 본래의 디자인을 유지하길 원한다. 그래서 주머니가 그대로 남았다. 다음에 그 작은 주머니를 보면, 그것이 한때는 <u>유용했다</u>는 것을 기억하라!

① **Have** you **seen** strange, tiny pockets [on your jeans]?
  ➜ have seen은 '본 적이 있다'의 의미로, 〈경험〉을 나타내는 현재완료(have[has]+p.p.)이다.
  ➜ [ ]는 tiny pockets를 수식하는 전치사구이다.
③ So, what are they **for**?
  ➜ for는 '~을 위해'의 의미로, 〈용도〉를 나타내는 전치사로 쓰였다.
⑨ Today **few people** carry pocket watches.
  ➜ few는 '거의 없는'의 부정의 의미로, 뒤에 셀 수 있는 명사의 복수형이 온다.
⑩ However, the company **wants to keep** the original design.
  ➜ 「want+to-v」는 '~하기를 원하다, ~하고 싶어 하다'의 의미이다.
⑪ So the pockets **have stayed**.
  ➜ have stayed는 '그대로 남았다'의 의미로, 〈계속〉을 나타내는 현재완료(have[has]+p.p.)이다.
⑫ The **next time** you see that little pocket, remember [(*that*) it was once useful]!
  ➜ 「next time ~」은 '다음에 ~할 때'의 의미이다.
  ➜ [ ]는 동사 remember의 목적어 역할을 하는 명사절로, 접속사 that이 생략되었다.

본책 • pp. 22-23

1 ②　　**2** ⑤　　**3** ④　　**4** 기린 개체 수를 증가시키는 것

1 기린을 보호하는 역할을 하는 호텔에 관한 소개 글이므로, 제목으로는 ② '투숙객과 기린을 위한 호텔'이 가장 알맞다.
　① 기린은 무엇을 먹는가?　　　　　　　　　③ 나이로비: 동물들에게 최고의 장소
　④ 로스차일드 기린은 왜 위험에 처했는가?　　⑤ 세계의 동물 친화적인 호텔들

2 ⑤: 문장 ⑪에서 투숙객이 기린에게 먹이를 줄 수 있다고 했다.
　①은 문장 ②에, ②는 문장 ⑤에, ③은 문장 ⑥에, ④는 문장 ⑩에 언급되어 있다.

3 기린의 개체 수를 증가시키기 위해 호텔이 기린을 서서히 야생으로 돌려보내고 있다는 내용 중에, 야생에서의 기린의 수명을 말하는 내용의 (d)는 흐름상 어색하다.

4 문장 ⑦을 통해 알 수 있다.
　Q: 그 호텔의 목적은 무엇인가?

① Do you love animals? / ② Then / this hotel in Nairobi, Kenya / is for you. / ③ It is
당신은 동물을 매우 좋아하는가　　그렇다면　케냐 나이로비에 있는 이 호텔은　　당신을 위한 것이다

next to a protected area / with a group of Rothschild's giraffes. / ④ These giraffes are
그것은 보호 구역 옆에 있다　　로스차일드 기린 무리가 있는　　이 기린들은 위험에

at risk / in the wild. / ⑤ The hotel was first built / in 1932. / ⑥ And / it started / to
처해 있다　야생에서　그 호텔은 최초로 건설되었다　1932년에　그리고　그것은 시작했다

protect giraffes / in the 1970s. / ⑦ The hotel's goal is / to increase the giraffe population. /
기린을 보호하는 것을　1970년대에　호텔의 목적은　기린 개체 수를 증가시키는 것이다

(⑧ Healthy giraffes can live / for 25 years / in the wild. /) ⑨ The hotel is slowly
건강한 기린은 살 수 있다　25년간　야생에서　호텔은 서서히 기린을

returning the giraffes / to the wild. / ⑩ Hotel guests can see the giraffes / up close. /
돌려보내고 있다　야생으로　호텔 투숙객은 기린을 볼 수 있다　바로 가까이에서

⑪ If they are lucky, / they can also feed them. / ⑫ Giraffes love to eat grass pellets /
그들이 운이 좋다면　그들은 그들에게 먹이를 줄 수도 있다　기린은 풀을 뭉친 알갱이를 먹는 것을 아주 좋아한다

at breakfast. / ⑬ Where else can you enjoy breakfast / with a giraffe? /
아침 식사 때　다른 어디에서 아침 식사를 즐길 수 있겠는가　기린과 함께

　　당신은 동물을 매우 좋아하는가? 그렇다면 케냐 나이로비에 있는 이 호텔은 당신을 위한 것이다. 그것은 로스차일드 기린 무리가 있는 보호 구역 옆에 있다. 이 기린들은 야생에서 위험에 처해 있다. 그 호텔은 1932년에 최초로 건설되었다. 그리고 1970년대에 기린을 보호하기 시작했다. 호텔의 목적은 기린 개체 수를 증가시키는 것이다. (건강한 기린은 야생에서 25년간 살 수 있다.) 호텔은 서서히 기린을 야생으로 돌려보내고 있다. 호텔 투숙객은 기린을 바로 가까이에서 볼 수 있다. 운이 좋다면, 그들에게 먹이를 줄 수도 있다. 기린은 아침 식사 때 풀을 뭉친 알갱이를 먹는 것을 아주 좋아한다. 다른 어디에서 기린과 함께 아침 식사를 즐길 수 있겠는가?

⑤ The hotel **was** first **built** in 1932.
➔ was built는 '건설되었다'의 의미로, 「be+p.p.」의 수동태이다.

⑦ The hotel's goal is **to increase** the giraffe population.
➔ to increase는 '증가시키는 것'의 의미로, 보어 역할을 하는 명사적 용법의 to부정사이다.

⑨ The hotel **is** slowly **returning** the giraffes to the wild.
➔ is returning은 '돌려보내고 있다'의 의미로, 「be동사의 현재형+v-ing」의 현재진행형이다.

⑪ **If** they are lucky, they can also feed them.
➔ if는 '만약 ~라면'의 의미로, 〈조건〉을 나타내는 접속사이다.

⑫ Giraffes **love to eat** grass pellets at breakfast.
➔ 「love+to-v[v-ing]」는 '~하는 것을 사랑하다[아주 좋아하다]'의 의미로, 목적어로 to부정사와 동명사 둘 다 쓸 수 있다.

Review Test

정답 **1** itchy **2** grass **3** vest **4** mosquito **5** feed **6** pocket **7** ⓐ **8** ⓒ **9** ⓑ
10 ⑤ **11** ⑤ **12** are at risk **13** deadly **14** come up with
15 The hotel's goal is to increase the giraffe population.
16 The company wants to keep the original design.
17 Think of the world's most dangerous animal.

문제 해설

1 itchy: 가려운

2 grass: 풀

3 vest: 조끼

4 mosquito: 모기

5 feed: 먹이를 주다

6 pocket: 주머니

7 bright(똑똑한, 영리한): ⓐ 똑똑하거나 총명한

8 goal(목표): ⓒ 성취하고 싶은 것

9 protect(보호하다): ⓑ 무언가를 해로운 것으로부터 안전하게 지키다

10 내가 음료를 다 마신 후 그 컵은 비었다.

① 형형색색의   ② 따뜻한   ③ 차분한   ④ 큰   ⑤ 가득 찬

11 아이들은 안전한 구역에서 놀고 있다.

① 운이 좋은   ② 유용한   ③ 낯선   ④ 원래의   ⑤ 위험한

12 be at risk: 위험에 처하다

13 deadly: 생명을 앗아가는, 치명적인

14 come up with: ~을 생각해 내다, (해답 등을) 찾아내다

15 '증가시키는 것'이라는 의미로, 명사적 용법의 to부정사 to increase를 문장의 보어로 쓴다.

16 '~하기를 원하다'라는 의미의 「want+to-v」를 쓴다.

17 '~해라'라는 의미로, 동사원형으로 문장을 시작하는 명령문 Think를 쓴다. dangerous는 3음절 이상의 형용사이므로 '가장 ~한'이라는 의미의 「most+형용사」를 최상급으로 쓴다.

SECTION 03

1

정답 1 ⑤   2 ②   3 (1) F (2) F   4 아시아의 코끼리는 더 습한 숲에 살기 때문에

문제 해설

1 코끼리의 주름이 수분을 보유하여 덥고 건조한 환경에서도 시원하게 지낼 수 있다는 내용의 글이므로, 제목으로는 ⑤ '코끼리가 어떻게 몸을 시원하게 유지하는가'가 가장 알맞다.
① 다양한 종류의 코끼리   ② 아프리카의 흥미로운 동물들
③ 주름의 다양한 목적   ④ 야생 코끼리를 보호하기 위한 노력

2 코끼리 피부의 주름이 더 많은 수분을 보유하여 건조해지는 데 시간이 더 걸린다는 내용 중에 코끼리가 한 번에 마실 수 있는 물의 양을 설명하는 (b)는 글의 흐름과 무관하다.

3 (1) 문장 ②, ④에서 코끼리는 캥거루와 같은 방법을 사용할 수 없다고 했다.
(2) 문장 ⑦-⑧에서 코끼리의 주름은 나이가 들었다는 의미가 아니며 어린 코끼리도 주름이 있다고 했다.

4 문장 ⑬에 언급되어 있다.

본문 직독 직해

① There are many ways / to stay cool / in the animal world. / ② Kangaroos lick / their
많은 방법들이 있다   시원하게 지내는   동물 세계에서   캥거루는 핥는다   그들의

arms. / ③ Dogs stick out / their tongues. / ④ But / elephants can't do either. / ⑤ They
팔을   개는 내민다   그들의 혀를   하지만 코끼리는 둘 중 어느 것도 할 수 없다   그들은

have other special ways / to keep cool. / ⑥ One is their wrinkly skin! / ⑦ The wrinkles
다른 특별한 방법들이 있다   시원하게 유지하는   한 가지는 그들의 주름이 있는 피부다   주름은 의미하지

don't mean / they are old! / ⑧ Even young elephants have them. / (⑨ Elephants can
않는다   그들이 나이가 들었다는 것을   어린 코끼리조차 그것들이 있다   코끼리는 마실 수 있다

drink / 200 liters of water / at one time.) ⑩ The wrinkles keep / five to ten times more
200ℓ의 물을   한 번에   주름은 보유한다   다섯 배에서 열 배 더 많은 수분을

water / than smooth skin. / ⑪ That means / it takes longer / for their skin / to dry out.
수분을   매끄러운 피부보다   그것은 의미한다   더 오래 걸린다는 것을   그들의 피부가   건조해지는 데

⑫ This is great / for staying cool longer / in hot and dry Africa. / ⑬ Elephants in Asia /
이는 아주 좋다   더 오래 시원하게 있기에   덥고 건조한 아프리카에서   아시아의 코끼리는

live in wetter forests, / so they have fewer wrinkles / than ones in Africa. /
더 습한 숲에 산다   그래서 그들은 주름이 더 적다   아프리카의 코끼리보다

본문 해석

동물 세계에는 시원하게 지내는 많은 방법들이 있다. 캥거루는 팔을 핥는다. 개는 혀를 내민다. 하지만 코끼리는 둘 중 어느 것도 할 수 없다. 그들은 시원하게 유지하는 다른 특별한 방법들이 있다. 한 가지는 그들의 주름이 있는 피부다! 주름은 그들이 나이가 들었다는 것을 의미하지 않는다! 어린 코끼리조차 그것들이 있다. (코끼리는 한 번에 200ℓ의 물을 마실 수 있다.) 주름은 매끄러운 피부보다 다섯 배에서 열 배 더 많은 수분을 보유한다. 그것은 그들의 피부가 건조해지는 데 더 오래 걸린다는 것을 의미한다. 이는 덥고 건조한 아프리카에서 더 오래 시원하게 있기에 아주 좋다. 아시아의 코끼리는 더 습한 숲에 살기 때문에 아프리카의 코끼리보다 주름이 더 적다.

구문 해설

① There are many ways **to stay cool** in the animal world.
➡ to stay cool은 명사구 many ways를 수식하는 형용사적 용법의 to부정사구이다.

④ But elephants can't do **either**.

➡ either는 부정문에서 '둘 중 어느 것도, 양쪽[두 개] 다 (아닌)'의 의미이다.

⑦ The wrinkles don't mean [(**that**) they are old]!

➡ [ ]는 동사 mean의 목적어 역할을 하는 명사절로, 접속사 that이 생략되었다.

⑩ The wrinkles keep **five to ten times more** water **than** smooth skin.

➡ 「배수사+비교급+than」은 '~보다 몇 배 더 …한'의 의미이다.

⑪ That means [(**that**) *it takes longer* <u>for their skin</u> *to dry out*].

➡ [ ]는 동사 means의 목적어 역할을 하는 명사절로, 접속사 that이 생략되었다.

➡ 「it takes+시간+to-v」는 '~하는 데 (시간이) 걸리다'의 의미이다. 여기서 it은 가주어이고, to부정사는 진주어이다.

➡ for their skin은 to부정사의 의미상의 주어이다.

⑫ This is great for **staying** cool longer in hot and dry Africa.

➡ staying은 전치사 for의 목적어 역할을 하는 동명사이다.

⑬ Elephants [in Asia] live in wetter forests, so they have **fewer wrinkles** than *ones* [in Africa].

➡ 두 개의 [ ]는 각각 앞의 명사 Elephants와 ones를 수식하는 전치사구이다.

➡ fewer는 '많지 않은, 적은'의 의미인 few의 비교급이다. few 뒤에는 셀 수 있는 명사의 복수형이 온다.

➡ ones는 elephants를 대신하며, 앞에 나온 명사의 반복을 피하기 위해 사용되었다.

본책 • pp. 30-31

정답 **1** ②   **2** ②   **3** (1) T (2) F   **4** popsicle, drink

문제 해설

1 아이스캔디가 어떻게 발명되었는지에 관한 글이므로, 주제로는 ② '최초의 아이스캔디 발명'이 가장 알맞다.

① 미국 아이들이 가장 좋아하는 간식   ③ 자신만의 아이스캔디 만드는 법

④ 가장 인기 있는 아이스캔디 맛   ⑤ Frank Epperson의 아이스캔디 사업

2 빈칸 뒤 단락에 우연히 아이스캔디를 발명하게 된 이야기가 나오고 있으므로, 빈칸에는 ② '실수'가 가장 알맞다.

① 노력 ③ 부모 ④ 숙제 ⑤ 사업

3 (1) 문장 ⑧에 언급되어 있다.

(2) 문장 ⑨에서 현관에 두었다고 했다.

4 | 보기 | 음료   막대기   아이스캔디   이야기

Frank Epperson이 하룻밤 동안 혼합된 <u>음료</u>를 현관에 두었을 때 최초의 <u>아이스캔디</u>를 만들었다.

본문 직독 직해

① A popsicle is a frozen treat / on a stick. / ② Many American kids enjoy it / in
아이스캔디는 얼린 간식이다   막대기에   많은 미국 아이들이 그것을 즐긴다

summer. / ③ Do you know / this treat's interesting story? / ④ Actually, / it came from
여름에   당신은 알고 있는가   이 간식의 흥미로운 이야기를   사실   그것은 한 아이의

a kid's mistake. /
실수에서 나왔다

⑤ It was winter / in 1905. / ⑥ Frank Epperson was 11 years old. / ⑦ He was making up
겨울이었다　　　1905년　　　Frank Epperson은 11살이었다　　　　　그는 음료수를 만들고

a drink. / ⑧ He mixed sweet soda powder and water / with a stick. / ⑨ He left his drink /
있었다　　　그는 달콤한 탄산음료 가루와 물을 섞었다　　　막대기로　　　그는 음료수를 두었다

on the porch / with the stick still in it. / ⑩ He completely forgot about it. / ⑪ He came
현관에　　　막대기가 여전히 들어있는 상태에서　　　그는 그것을 완전히 잊어버렸다　　　그는

back / the next day. / ⑫ The drink was frozen! / ⑬ But he didn't throw it away. /
돌아왔다　다음 날　　　　음료수는 얼어 있었다　　　그러나 그는 그것을 버리지 않았다

⑭ Instead, / he licked it. / ⑮ Wow! / ⑯ It was delicious. / ⑰ The first popsicle was born. /
대신에　　　그는 그것을 핥았다　　와　　　그것은 맛있었다　　　첫 번째 아이스캔디가 탄생했다

본문 해석

아이스캔디는 막대기에 얼린 간식이다. 많은 미국 아이들이 여름에 그것을 즐긴다. 당신은 이 간식의 흥미로운 이야기를 알고 있는가? 사실, 그것은 한 아이의 실수에서 나왔다.

1905년 겨울이었다. Frank Epperson은 11살이었다. 그는 음료수를 만들고 있었다. 그는 막대기로 달콤한 탄산음료 가루와 물을 섞었다. 그는 막대기가 여전히 들어있는 상태에서 음료수를 현관에 두었다. 그는 그것을 완전히 잊어버렸다. 그는 다음 날 돌아왔다. 음료수는 얼어 있었다! 그러나 그는 그것을 버리지 않았다. 대신에, 그는 그것을 핥았다. 와! 그것은 맛있었다. 첫 번째 아이스캔디가 탄생했다.

구문 해설

⑦ He **was making** up a drink.
　➡ was making은 '만들고 있었다'의 의미로, 「be동사의 과거형+v-ing」의 과거진행형이다.

⑨ He left his drink on the porch **with the stick still** in *it*.
　➡ 「with+명사+부사」는 '~을 …한 채로'의 의미이다.
　➡ it은 his drink를 가리킨다.

⑬ But he didn't **throw it away**.
　➡ throw away는 「동사+부사」로 이루어진 동사구로, 목적어가 대명사일 경우 동사와 부사 사이에 쓴다.

⑰ The first popsicle **was born**.
　➡ was born은 '탄생했다'의 의미로, 「be+p.p.」의 수동태이다.

본책 ● pp. 32-33

3

정답　1 ⑤　2 ⑤　3 ③　4 ②

문제 해설

1　발리 사람들이 새해를 기념하는 날인 녜삐에 관한 글이므로, 주제로는 ⑤가 가장 알맞다.

2　문장 ⑧, ⑩에서 녜삐에 사람들이 어떠한 소리도 내지 않고 비행기가 날지 않으며 식당도 열지 않는다고 했으므로, 빈칸에는 ⑤ '침묵'이 가장 알맞다.
　① 재미　② 소음　③ 공포　④ 슬픔

3　③: 문장 ⑥에서 오전 6시에 시작해서 24시간 동안 계속된다고 했으므로 다음 날 오전 6시에 끝난다.
　①은 문장 ②-③에, ②는 문장 ⑤에, ④는 문장 ⑨에, ⑤는 문장 ⑩에 언급되어 있다.

4　문장 ⑫-⑬에 언급되어 있다.
　Q: 사람들은 왜 녜삐에 조용히 실내에 머무는가?

본문
직독
직해

① Most people around the world / have lively New Year's parties. / ② But / the
세계 대부분의 사람들이　　　　　　활기 넘치는 새해 파티를 한다　　　　　그러나

Balinese welcome their New Year / differently. / ③ They celebrate it / with Nyepi! /
발리 사람들은 그들의 새해를 맞이한다　　　다르게　　　그들은 그것을 기념한다　네삐로

④ Nyepi is a day / of silence. / ⑤ It takes place / on the first day / of the Balinese *saka*
네삐는 날이다　　침묵의　　　그것은 이루어진다　　첫날에　　　발리식 '사카' 달력의

calendar. / ⑥ It starts / at 6 a.m. / and continues / for 24 hours. / ⑦ On this day, / people
　　　그것은 시작한다　오전 6시에　그리고 계속된다　24시간 동안　　　이날　　　사람들은

clear their minds. / ⑧ They don't make any noise. / ⑨ This helps / keep the balance /
마음을 깨끗하게 한다　　그들은 어떠한 소리도 내지 않는다　　이는 돕는다　　균형을 유지하는 것을

between nature and humans. / ⑩ No planes fly / and no restaurants open. / ⑪ People
자연과 인간 사이의　　　　비행기가 날지 않는다　그리고 식당은 열지 않는다　　　사람들은

should stay indoors / on Nyepi. / ⑫ The Balinese think / demons will be fooled / if all is
실내에 머물러야 한다　　네삐에　　　발리 사람들은 생각한다　　악령이 속을 거라고　　　모두가

quiet / on Nyepi. / ⑬ The demons will think / no one is there / and leave. / ⑭ This will
조용하면　네삐에　　　악령은 생각할 것이다　　그곳에 아무도 없다고　그리고 떠날 것이다　이것이

bring / good luck and peace / to Bali. /
가져다줄 것이다　행운과 평화를　　　발리에

본문
해석

　세계 대부분의 사람들이 활기 넘치는 새해 파티를 한다. 그러나 발리 사람들은 새해를 다르게 맞이한다. 그들은 네삐로 새해를 기념한다!

　네삐는 침묵의 날이다. 그것은 발리식 '사카' 달력의 첫날에 이루어진다. 그것은 오전 6시에 시작해서 24시간 동안 계속된다. 이날, 사람들은 마음을 깨끗하게 한다. 그들은 어떠한 소리도 내지 않는다. 이는 자연과 인간 사이의 균형을 유지하는 것을 돕는다. 비행기가 날지 않고 식당은 열지 않는다. 네삐에 사람들은 실내에 머물러야 한다. 발리 사람들은 네삐에 모두가 조용하면 악령이 속을 거라고 생각한다. 악령은 그곳에 아무도 없다고 생각해서 떠날 것이다. 이것이 발리에 행운과 평화를 가져다줄 것이다.

구문
해설

① **Most people** [around the world] **have** lively New Year's parties.
　➡ 문장의 주어인 Most people이 복수 명사이므로, 복수형 동사 have가 쓰였다.
　➡ [ ]는 Most people을 수식하는 전치사구이다.

⑥ It **starts** at 6 a.m. and **continues** for 24 hours.
　➡ 문장의 동사 starts와 continues가 접속사 and로 병렬 연결되어 있다.

⑨ This **helps keep** the balance between nature and humans.
　➡ 「help+동사원형[to-v]」은 '~하는 것을 돕다'의 의미이다.

⑫ The Balinese think [(**that**) demons will be fooled *if* all is quiet on Nyepi].
　➡ [ ]는 동사 think의 목적어 역할을 하는 명사절로, 접속사 that이 생략되었다.
　➡ if는 '만약 ~라면'의 의미로, 〈조건〉을 나타내는 접속사이다.

⑬ The demons will **think** [(*that*) no one is there] and **leave**.
　➡ 동사원형 think와 leave가 접속사 and로 병렬 연결되어 있다.
　➡ [ ]는 think의 목적어 역할을 하는 명사절로, 접속사 that이 생략되었다.

⑭ This will **bring** good luck and peace **to** Bali.
　➡ 「bring A to B」는 'B에게 A를 가져다주다'의 의미로, 「bring B A」로 바꿔 쓸 수 있다.

정답 **1** lick **2** wrinkle **3** calendar **4** powder **5** nature **6** frozen **7** © **8** ⓐ
9 ⓑ **10** ② **11** ⑤ **12** take place **13** was born **14** stick out
15 He was making up a drink.
16 This helps keep the balance between nature and humans.
17 it takes longer for their skin to dry out

문제 해설

1 lick: 핥다

2 wrinkle: 주름

3 calendar: 달력

4 powder: 가루

5 nature: 자연

6 frozen: 냉동된

7 mistake(실수): © 무심코 잘못한 일

8 lively(활기 넘치는): ⓐ 흥미나 에너지로 가득 찬

9 forest(숲): ⓑ 많은 나무가 있는 넓은 지역

10 비는 땅을 젖게 만들었다.

  ① 달콤한   ② 마른   ③ 시원한   ④ 매끈한   ⑤ 흥미로운

11 불을 꺼야 하는 것을 잊지 마세요.

  ① 떠나다   ② 유지하다   ③ 계속하다   ④ 가져다주다   ⑤ 기억하다

12 take place: 개최되다, 일어나다

13 be born: 태어나다

14 stick out: ~을 내밀다

15 '~하고 있었다'라는 의미의 「be동사의 과거형+v-ing」 형태의 과거진행형을 쓴다.

16 '~하는 것을 돕다'라는 의미의 「help+동사원형」을 쓴다.

17 '~하는 데 (시간이) 걸리다'라는 의미의 「it takes+시간+to-v」를 쓴다. to부정사 앞에는 의미상의 주어인 for their skin을 쓴다.

SECTION 04

1

정답 1 ② 2 ⑤ 3 양 무릎을 꿇어야 한다. 4 chin, lose

문제 해설

1 '다운 다운 다운'이라는 게임을 하는 방식에 관한 글이므로, 주제로는 ② '한 재미있는 게임의 규칙'이 가장 알맞다.
① 대중 스포츠의 기원
③ 함께 운동하는 쉬운 방법
④ 한 게임의 이름이 유래된 곳
⑤ 부정행위를 하지 않고 게임을 이기는 방법

2 약 10걸음 정도 떨어져 서라는 내용 뒤에, 테니스공을 왔다 갔다 던지라는 내용의 (C), 오랫동안 그 공을 떨어뜨리지 않으면, 각 선수가 한 걸음 뒤로 물러나야 한다는 내용의 (B), 그러나 그 공을 떨어뜨리면, 한 쪽 무릎을 꿇고 앉아야 한다는 내용의 (A)로 이어지는 흐름이 가장 알맞다.

3 문장 ⑨를 통해 알 수 있다.

> Q: 만약 당신이 공을 두 번 떨어뜨리면 무엇을 해야 하는가?

4 문장 ⑪-⑫를 통해 알 수 있다.

> 지면에 닿는 마지막 신체 부위는 턱이다. 그 뒤에 공을 떨어뜨리면 경기에서 진다.

본문 직독 직해

① Let's play a fun game. / ② It's called / Down, Down, Down. / ③ First, / find a
재미있는 게임을 해보자   그것은 불린다   다운, 다운, 다운이라고   먼저   짝을

partner. / ④ Stand about 10 steps away / from each other. / ⑦ Then / gently throw a
찾아라   약 10걸음 정도 떨어져 서라   서로로부터   그리고 나서 부드럽게 테니스공을

tennis ball / back and forth. / ⑥ If no one drops the ball / for a long time, / each player
던져라   왔다 갔다   만약 아무도 그 공을 떨어뜨리지 않으면   오랫동안   각 선수는

takes a step back. / ⑤ However, / if you drop the ball, / you must go down / on one
한 걸음 뒤로 물러난다   하지만   당신이 그 공을 떨어뜨리면   당신은 꿇어야 한다   한쪽

knee. / ⑧ Then / the game continues. / ⑨ On the second drop, / you must kneel / on
무릎을   그리고   게임은 계속된다   두 번째로 떨어뜨릴 때   당신은 꿇어야 한다

both knees. / ⑩ After that, / you have to place one elbow / on the floor / and then put
양 무릎을   그 후   당신은 한쪽 팔꿈치를 놓아야 한다   바닥에   그리고 다음에는

down the other. / ⑪ The final body part / to go down / is the chin. / ⑫ If you drop the
다른 쪽을 내려놓아야 한다.   마지막 신체 부위는   아래로 내려갈   턱이다   만약 당신이 다시 그 공을

ball again, / you lose the game. /
떨어뜨리면   당신은 게임에서 지게 된다

본문 해석

재미있는 게임을 해보자. 그것은 다운, 다운, 다운이라고 불린다. 먼저, 짝을 찾아라. 서로 약 10걸음 정도 떨어져 서라. (C) 그리고 나서 왔다 갔다 부드럽게 테니스공을 던져라. (B) 만약 아무도 오랫동안 그 공을 떨어뜨리지 않으면, 각 선수는 한 걸음 뒤로 물러난다. (A) 하지만, 당신이 그 공을 떨어뜨리면, 한쪽 무릎을 꿇어야 한다. 그리고 게임은 계속된다. 두 번째로 떨어뜨릴 때, 당신은 양 무릎을 꿇어야 한다. 그 후, 한쪽 팔꿈치를 바닥에 놓고 그 다음에는 다른 쪽 팔꿈치를 내려놓아야 한다. 아래로 내려갈 마지막 신체 부위는 턱이다. 만약 당신이 한 번 더 그 공을 떨어뜨리면, 당신은 게임에서 지게 된다.

② It**'s called** Down, Down, Down.

→ 「A be called B」는 'A는 B라고 불린다'의 의미이다.

⑥ **If** no one drops the ball for a long time, *each player takes* a step back.

→ if는 '만약 ~라면'의 의미로, 〈조건〉을 나타내는 접속사이다.

→ 「each+단수 명사」는 '각각의 ~'의 의미로, 단수 취급하므로 단수형 동사 takes가 쓰였다.

⑩ After **that**, you have to place *one* elbow on the floor and then put down *the other* (*elbow*).

→ that은 앞 문장에서 언급한 두 번째로 공을 떨어뜨려 양 무릎을 꿇은 것을 가리킨다.

→ 대상이 두 가지로 정해져 있을 때 둘 중 하나는 one으로, 다른 하나는 the other로 나타낸다. 여기에서는 사람의 팔꿈치가 두 개이므로 one과 the other를 썼으며, 반복을 피하기 위해 the other 뒤에 elbow가 생략되었다.

⑪ The final body part **to go** down is the chin.

→ to go는 '갈'의 의미로, 명사구 The final body part를 수식하는 형용사적 용법의 to부정사이다.

본책 • pp. 40-41

2

정답   1 ④   2 뜨거운 차가 (콧수염의) 왁스를 녹이거나 콧수염을 젖게 할 수 있었다.   3 ⑤   4 (1) T (2) F

**문제
해설**

1 뜨거운 차를 마시는 동안 콧수염을 보호할 수 있도록 발명된 컵에 대한 글이므로, 주제로는 ④ '콧수염을 위한 컵의 발명'이 가장 알맞다.

① 영국의 차 문화

② 왁스가 왜 피부에 좋지 않은가

③ 영국 신사들의 패션 스타일

⑤ 1800년대에 남성들은 왜 콧수염을 길렀는가

2 문장 ⑤를 통해 알 수 있다.

Q: 콧수염이 있는 남성들이 뜨거운 차를 즐길 때 어떤 문제가 있었는가?

3 문장 ⑨-⑩을 통해 알 수 있다.

4 (1) 문장 ⑦-⑧에 언급되어 있다.

(2) 문장 ⑬에서 콧수염 컵이 유럽 전역에서 인기를 얻었다고 했다.

**본문
직독
직해**

① In the mid-19th century, / most men grew mustaches. / ② They wanted / to keep
　19세기 중반에　　　　　　　대부분의 남성들은 콧수염을 길렀다　　　그들은 원했다　　　그들의

their mustaches neat. / ③ So / they often used wax. /
콧수염을 단정하게 유지하는 것을　　그래서 그들은 흔히 왁스를 사용했다

④ However, / this made enjoying tea difficult. / ⑤ Hot tea could melt the wax / or
그러나　　　이는 차를 즐기는 것을 어렵게 만들었다　　　뜨거운 차가 왁스를 녹일 수도 있었다　　또는

get their mustaches wet. / ⑥ It was a big problem / for them. / ⑦ Harvey Adams, a
그들의 콧수염을 젖게 할 수도 있었다　　이는 큰 문제였다　　　그들에게　　　영국의 도예가

British potter, / had an idea. / ⑧ In England during the 1860s, / he invented / the
Harvey Adams는　　아이디어가 떠올랐다　　1860년대 영국에서　　　그는 발명했다

mustache cup! / ⑨ This special cup had / a small barrier. / ⑩ It protected the mustache /
콧수염 컵을　　　　이 특별한 컵은 가지고 있었다　작은 가림막을　　　그것은 콧수염을 보호했다

by covering it. / ⑪ It also had a small hole / to drink through. /
그것을 가림으로써　　　그것은 작은 구멍도 가지고 있었다　통해 마실 수 있는

⑫ Finally / a gentleman could have a handsome mustache / and enjoy his tea time. /
마침내　　신사는 멋진 콧수염을 가질 수 있었다　　　　그리고 차를 마시는 시간을 즐길 수 있었다

⑬ Soon / mustache cups became popular / all over Europe. /
곧　　　콧수염 컵은 인기를 얻게 되었다　　　유럽 전역에서

본문 해석

19세기 중반에, 대부분의 남성들은 콧수염을 길렀다. 그들은 콧수염을 단정하게 유지하기를 원했다. 그래서 그들은 흔히 왁스를 사용했다.

그러나, 이는 차를 즐기는 것을 어렵게 만들었다. 뜨거운 차가 왁스를 녹이거나 콧수염을 젖게 할 수도 있었다. 이는 그들에게 큰 문제였다. 영국의 도예가 Harvey Adams는 아이디어가 떠올랐다. 1860년대 영국에서 그는 콧수염 컵을 발명했다! 이 특별한 컵에는 작은 가림막이 있었다. 그것은 콧수염을 가려서 그것을 보호했다. (구멍을) 통해 마실 수 있는 작은 구멍도 있었다.

마침내 신사는 멋진 콧수염을 가지고 차를 마시는 시간을 즐길 수 있었다. 곧 콧수염 컵은 유럽 전역에서 인기를 얻게 되었다.

구문 해설

④ However, this **made enjoying tea difficult**.
→ 「make+목적어+형용사」는 '~을 …하게 만들다'의 의미이다. 여기서는 동명사구 enjoying tea가 목적어로 쓰였다.

⑤ Hot tea **could melt** the wax or (**could**) **get** their mustaches wet.
→ could melt와 (could) get이 접속사 or로 병렬 연결되어 있다.
→ 「get+목적어+형용사」는 '~을 …하게 만들다'의 의미이다.

⑦ **Harvey Adams**, **a British potter**, had an idea.
→ Harvey Adams와 a British potter는 동격 관계로, 콤마(,)는 동격을 나타낸다.

⑪ It also had a small hole **to drink through**.
→ to drink through는 '(통해) 마시는'의 의미로, 명사구 a small hole을 수식하는 형용사적 용법의 to부정사구이다. drink through a small hole의 의미이므로 뒤에 전치사 through가 쓰였다.

⑬ Soon mustache cups **became popular** all over Europe.
→ 「become+형용사」는 '~하게 되다'의 의미이다.

본책 • pp. 42-43

3

정답　　1 ③　　2 ④　　3 (1) T (2) F　　4 portraits

문제 해설

1　주세페 아르침볼도가 다양한 사물들을 활용하는 방식으로 재미있는 초상화를 그렸다는 내용의 글이므로, 제목으로는 ③ '초상화를 만드는 창의적인 방법'이 가장 알맞다.
① 자화상을 그리는 방법　　　　　　② 16세기의 그림들
④ 르네상스 미술의 진정한 아름다움　　　⑤ 화가들은 왜 채소 그리기를 좋아하는가

2　여러 채소들로 이루어진 초상화를 묘사하는 내용 중에, 채소에서 건강에 좋은 비타민을 얻을 수 있다는 내용의 (d)는 글의 흐름과 무관하다.

3 (1) 문장 ③에 언급되어 있다.

(2) 문장 ⑫에서 파스닙으로 코를, 버섯으로 입술을 표현했다고 했다.

4 문장 ④, ⑦을 통해 알 수 있다.

> 주세페 아르침볼도는 무작위의 사물을 그려서 <u>초상화</u>를 만들었다.

당신은 르네상스 미술이 매우 지루하다고 생각할지도 모른다. 하지만 주세페 아르침볼도의 작품은 재미있다. 그는 16세기 화가였다. 그는 몇 점의 재미있는 초상화를 그렸다. 멀리서 보면, 그것들은 사람처럼 보인다. 하지만 가까이서 보라! 그 사람들은 음식, 꽃, 그리고 책과 같은 다양한 사물들로 이루어져 있다.

그의 작품 중 한 예는 〈채소 기르는 사람〉이다. 그것은 그릇에 담긴 채소 그림이다. (채소로부터 건강에 좋은 비타민을 얻을 수 있다.) 그 그림을 거꾸로 돌리면, 어떤 사람이 당신을 보고 미소 짓고 있다! 양파는 통통한 볼이고, 큰 파스닙은 긴 코이고, 버섯은 입술이다. 당신은 당신의 초상화에 어떤 사물을 사용하겠는가?

① You **might** think [(*that*) Renaissance art is very boring].
- → might는 '~할지도 모른다'의 의미인 조동사로, 〈추측〉을 나타낸다.
- → [ ]는 동사 think의 목적어 역할을 하는 명사절로, 접속사 that이 생략되었다.

⑤ From a distance, they **look like** people.
- → 「look like ~」는 '~처럼 보이다'의 의미로, 뒤에 명사가 온다.

⑦ Those people **are made of** various items *such as* food, flowers, and books.
- → 「be made of ~」는 '~로 구성되다, ~로 만들어지다'의 의미이다.
- → 「such as ~」는 '~와 같은'의 의미로, 뒤에 예시에 해당하는 내용이 이어진다.

⑬ **Which items** would you use for your portrait?
- → 「which+명사」는 '어떤[무슨] ~'의 의미이다.

정답
1 vegetable　**2** potter　**3** throw　**4** player　**5** upside down　**6** cover　**7** ⓑ
8 ⓐ　**9** ⓒ　**10** ③　**11** ⑤　**12** barrier　**13** from a distance　**14** back and forth
15 The final body part to go down is the chin.
16 Which items would you use for your portrait?
17 This made enjoying tea difficult.

문제 해설

1　vegetable: 채소

2　potter: 도예가

3　throw: 던지다

4　player: 참가자[선수]

5　upside down: 거꾸로

6　cover: (보호하기 위해) 가리다, 씌우다

7　creative(창조적인, 창의적인): ⓑ 새로운 아이디어를 내는 것을 잘하는

8　neat(정돈된, 단정한, 깔끔한): ⓐ 깨끗하고 깔끔한

9　origin(기원, 근원): ⓒ 무언가가 유래한 곳

10　나의 고양이는 많이 먹어서 <u>뚱뚱해졌다.</u>
　　① 지루한　　② 깔끔한　　③ 마른　　④ 건강한　　⑤ 큰

11　그 선수들은 지쳐서 경기에서 <u>질지도</u> 모른다.
　　① 자라다　　② 발명하다　　③ 떨어뜨리다　　④ 무릎을 꿇다　　⑤ 이기다

12　barrier: 장벽, 벽

13　from a distance: 멀리서, 멀리 떨어져서

14　back and forth: 왔다 갔다

15　'내려갈'이라는 의미로, 명사구 The final body part를 수식하는 형용사적 용법의 to부정사구 to go down을 쓴다.

16　'어떤[무슨] ~'이라는 의미의 「which+명사」를 쓴다.

17　'~을 …하게 만들다'라는 의미의 「make+목적어+형용사」를 쓴다.

SECTION 05

1

정답　　**1** ⑤　**2** ②　**3** ②　**4** (1) hurt　(2) unique

문제 해설

1 비문이 개의 신원 확인에 효과적임을 설명하는 내용의 글이므로, 제목으로는 ⑤ '비문: 개의 신원을 확인하는 최고의 방법'이 가장 알맞다.
① 캐나다의 잃어버린 개들　　　　　② 개들은 왜 냄새를 잘 맡을 수 있는가?
③ 개의 비문을 등록하는 방법　　　　④ 마이크로칩이 개들에게 왜 좋은가

2 문장 ②에서 각 개의 비문은 유일무이하다고 했으며, 빈칸 뒤 문장에서 캐나다에서 사람들은 개의 신원을 확인하기 위해 비문을 이용한다고 했으므로, 빈칸에는 ② '찾다'가 가장 알맞다.
① 산책시키다　③ 피하다　④ 기르다　⑤ 기억하다

3 개의 신원을 확인하는 방법으로 비문의 장점을 설명하는 내용 중에, 개가 인간보다 더 민감한 코를 가졌다고 말하는 내용의 (b)는 흐름상 어색하다.

4 <u>보기</u> │ 유일무이한　변하다　똑같은　아프게 하다

개의 신원을 확인하는 방법

꼬리표와 목걸이	마이크로칩	비문
쉽게 분실될 수 있다.	개의 몸속에 넣으면 개를 (1) <u>아프게 할</u> 수 있다.	각 개에게 (2) <u>유일무이하다</u>. 채취하기 쉽다.

본문 직독 직해

① Every fingerprint is unique. / ② Each dog's nose print is unique too! / ③ Look at
　모든 지문은 유일무이하다　　　　각 개의 비문도 유일무이하다

a dog's nose / closely. / ④ You can see lines. / ⑤ They can help us / find lost dogs. / ⑥ In
개의 코를 보아라　주의해서　　선들을 볼 수 있다　　그것들이 우리를 도울 수 있다　잃어버린 개를 찾도록

Canada, / people already use / these patterns / to identify dogs. /
캐나다에서　사람들은 이미 이용한다　이 무늬를　　개의 신원을 확인하기 위해

⑦ Tags and collars / are often used, / but they can be lost or stolen. / ⑧ Some owners
　꼬리표와 목걸이가　흔히 사용된다　하지만 그것들은 분실되거나 도난당할 수 있다　어떤 견주들은

also use / microchips. / ⑨ They are put / inside dogs. / ⑩ This can hurt them. /
또한 사용한다　마이크로칩을　그것들은 넣어진다　개의 몸속에　　이는 그들을 아프게 할 수 있다

⑪ Microchips can also break. / ⑫ So, many people think / nose prints are better. /
마이크로칩은 또한 부서질 수 있다　그래서 많은 사람들이 생각한다　비문이 더 낫다고

(⑬ Dogs have more sensitive noses / than humans.) ⑭ Dogs' nose prints don't
　개는 더 민감한 코를 가지고 있다　　인간보다　　　개의 비문은 변하지 않는다

change / as dogs get older. / ⑮ They can't be removed either! / ⑯ Also it's easy and
변하지　개가 나이가 들면서　　그것들은 제거될 수도 없다　　또한 쉽고 고통이 없다

painless / to collect nose prints. / ⑰ So, / dog owners, / hurry up / and register them! /
비문을 채취하는 것은　　그러니　견주들이여　서둘러라　그리고 그것들을 등록하라

본문
해석

　모든 지문은 유일무이하다. 각 개의 비문도 유일무이하다! 개의 코를 주의해서 보아라. 선들을 볼 수 있다. 그것들은 우리가 잃어버린 개를 찾는 것을 도울 수 있다. 캐나다에서 사람들은 이미 개의 신원을 확인하기 위해 이 무늬를 이용한다.

　꼬리표와 목걸이가 흔히 사용되지만, 그것들은 분실되거나 도난당할 수 있다. 어떤 견주들은 또한 마이크로칩을 사용한다. 그것들은 개의 몸속에 넣어진다. 이는 그들을 아프게 할 수 있다. 마이크로칩은 또한 부서질 수 있다. 그래서 많은 사람들이 비문이 더 낫다고 생각한다. (개는 인간보다 더 민감한 코를 가지고 있다.) 개의 비문은 개가 나이가 들면서 변하지 않는다. 그것들은 제거될 수도 없다! 또한 비문을 채취하는 것은 쉽고 고통이 없다. 그러니 견주들이여, 서둘러서 비문을 등록하라!

구문
해설

③ **Look** at a dog's nose closely.
　➜ 동사원형 Look이 문장 맨 앞에 와서 명령문으로 쓰였다.

⑤ They can **help us find** lost dogs.
　➜ 「help+목적어+동사원형[to-v]」은 '~가 …하는 것을 돕다'의 의미이다.

⑥ In Canada, people already use these patterns **to identify** dogs.
　➜ to identify는 '신원을 확인하기 위해'라는 의미로, 〈목적〉을 나타내는 부사적 용법의 to부정사이다.

⑦ Tags and collars are often used, but they can **be lost** or (**be**) **stolen**.
　➜ be lost와 (be) stolen은 각각 '분실되다'와 '도난당하다'의 의미로, 「be+p.p.」의 수동태이다. 이 둘은 접속사 or로 병렬 연결되어 있다.

⑫ So, many people think [(**that**) nose prints are better].
　➜ [ ]는 동사 think의 목적어 역할을 하는 명사절로, 접속사 that이 생략되었다.

⑭ Dogs' nose prints don't change **as** dogs get older.
　➜ as는 '~함에 따라'의 의미로 쓰인 접속사이다.

⑮ They can't be removed **either**!
　➜ either는 '~도 (그렇다)'의 의미로 주로 부정문에서 쓰인다.

⑯ Also **it**'s easy and painless **to collect nose prints**.
　➜ it은 가주어이고, to collect nose prints가 진주어이다.

본책 • pp. 50-51

정답　**1** ④　**2** ③　**3** (1) T (2) T　**4** superstition, whistles

**문제
해설**

1　극장에서 휘파람을 불면 안 된다는 미신이 생긴 배경을 설명하는 글이므로, 주제로는 ④가 가장 알맞다.

2　무대 담당자들이 현재 헤드폰을 사용함에 따라 관객의 휘파람이 더 이상 사고를 일으키지 않지만, 여전히 극장에서 휘파람을 불면 안 된다는 관습이 있다는 내용으로, 빈칸에는 ③ '남아 있다'가 가장 알맞다.
　① 시작된다　② 문제가 된다　④ 바뀐다　⑤ 사라진다

3　(1) 문장 ④에 언급되어 있다.
　(2) 문장 ⑩에 언급되어 있다.

4　| 보기 | 미신　배경　관객　휘파람 |

한 미신은 우리가 극장에서 휘파람을 불면 안 된다고 한다. 그것은 무대 담당자들이 휘파람을 신호로 사용했기 때문이다.

① Do you think / all superstitions are silly? / ② Well, / some started / for good
당신은 생각하는가　　모든 미신이 어리석다고　　　　　　그런데　　일부는 시작되었다　　타당한

reasons! / ③ Take this superstition / for example: / you should never whistle / in a
이유에서　　　　이 미신을 들어보자　　　　　예로　　　　당신은 절대 휘파람을 불면 안 된다

theater. / ④ A long time ago, / theater backgrounds were large paintings. /
극장에서　　　　오래전에　　　　　　극장의 배경은 커다란 그림들이었다

⑤ Stagehands raised and lowered them / with ropes. / ⑥ To tell each other / to pull or
무대 담당자들이 그것들을 올리고 내렸다　　　　밧줄로　　　　　서로에게 말하기 위해　　밧줄을 당기거나

loosen the ropes, / they whistled. / ⑦ Whistles from the audience / sometimes confused
느슨하게 하라고　　　그들은 휘파람을 불었다　　관객에게서 나오는 휘파람은　　　　때때로 그들을 혼란스럽게 했다

them! / ⑧ The background could be dropped / onto an actor. / ⑨ Ouch! /
배경이 떨어질 수도 있었다　　　　　　배우에게　　　　아야

⑩ These days / stagehands use headsets. / ⑪ Whistles don't cause accidents /
오늘날　　　　무대 담당자들은 헤드폰을 이용한다　　　휘파람은 사고를 일으키지 않는다

any more. / ⑫ However, / the custom remains. / ⑬ This is why / you should not whistle /
더 이상　　　　그러나　　　그 관습은 남아 있다　　　이것이 ~한 이유이다　당신이 휘파람을 불면 안 되는

at the theater. /
극장에서

　　당신은 모든 미신이 어리석다고 생각하는가? 그런데, 일부는 타당한 이유에서 시작되었다! 이 미신을 예로 들
어보자. 극장에서는 절대 휘파람을 불면 안 된다. 오래전에, 극장의 배경은 커다란 그림들이었다. 무대 담당자들이
밧줄로 그것들을 올리고 내렸다. 밧줄을 당기거나 느슨하게 하라고 서로에게 말하기 위해, 그들은 휘파람을 불었다.
관객에게서 나오는 휘파람은 때때로 그들을 혼란스럽게 했다! 배경이 배우에게 떨어질 수도 있었다. 아야!
　　오늘날 무대 담당자들은 헤드폰을 이용한다. 휘파람은 더 이상 사고를 일으키지 않는다. 그러나 그 관습은 남
아 있다. 이것이 극장에서 휘파람을 불면 안 되는 이유이다.

① Do you think [(**that**) all superstitions are silly]?
　➔ [ ]는 동사 think의 목적어 역할을 하는 명사절로, 접속사 that이 생략되었다.

② Well, **some** started for good reasons!
　➔ some은 some superstitions를 가리킨다.

⑥ **To tell** *each other to pull or (to) loosen* the ropes, they whistled.
　➔ To tell은 '말하기 위해'의 의미로, 〈목적〉을 나타내는 부사적 용법의 to부정사이다.
　➔ 「tell+목적어+to-v」는 '~에게 …하라고 말하다'의 의미로, to pull과 (to) loosen이 접속사 or로 병렬 연결되
　　어 있다.

⑦ **Whistles** [from the audience] sometimes **confused** them!
　➔ 전치사구 [ ]의 수식을 받는 Whistles가 주어이고, confused가 동사이다.

⑪ Whistles do**n't** cause accidents **any more**.
　➔ 「not ~ any more」는 '더 이상 ~ 않다'의 의미를 나타낸다.

⑬ **This is why** you should not whistle at the theater.
　➔ 「this is why ~」는 '이것이 ~한 이유이다'의 의미로, 뒤에 결과에 해당하는 내용이 온다.

3

정답 **1** ② **2** ③ **3** ⑤ **4** ground, gardens

문제 해설

1 도시들이 건물에 야외 정원을 조성하고 있다는 내용의 글이므로, 제목으로는 ② '땅 위 높은 곳에 있는 정원'이 가장 알맞다.
① 숲을 사라지게 만드는 것 ③ 대도시 근처의 숲 보호하기
④ 수직의 숲: 실내 정원 가꾸기 ⑤ 도시 지역의 지하 농장

2 ③: 바람으로부터 건물을 보호한다는 것은 언급되지 않았다.
①은 문장 ④에, ②는 문장 ⑤에 ④와 ⑤는 문장 ⑥에 언급되어 있다.

3 '그것은 보스코 베르티칼레라고 불린다'라는 문장은 가장 유명한 녹색 고층 건물 중 하나가 이탈리아 밀라노에 있다는 내용의 문장 ⑩과 그것의 이름의 의미를 설명하는 문장 ⑪ 사이인 ⑤의 위치가 가장 알맞다.

4 문장 ②와 ⑧에 언급되어 있다.

> 도시에는 식물과 나무를 위한 땅 위의 공간이 거의 없기 때문에 건축가들은 야외 정원이 있는 건물을 설계하고 있다.

본문 직독 직해

① Most cities are crowded. / ② There is little space / for trees and plants / on the
대부분의 도시들은 붐빈다   공간이 거의 없다   나무와 식물을 위한   땅 위에

ground. / ③ But / cities need plants and trees. / ④ They clean the air. / ⑤ They also
          하지만 도시는 식물과 나무가 필요하다   그것들은 공기를 깨끗하게 한다   그것들은 또한

prevent flooding / by absorbing rain. / ⑥ Sometimes, / they provide homes for animals /
홍수를 방지한다   빗물을 흡수함으로써   때때로   그것들은 동물들에게 서식지를 제공한다

and help people relax. / ⑦ So / people in cities have found a new place / for plants and
그리고 사람들을 휴식하도록 돕는다   그래서 도시의 사람들은 새로운 장소를 찾았다   식물과 나무를 위한

trees / — high above their heads. / ⑧ Architects are now designing buildings / with
          바로 머리 위 높은 곳이다   건축가들은 현재 건물을 설계하고 있다

outdoor gardens. / ⑨ Hundreds of plants and trees can be grown / in these gardens. /
야외 정원이 있는   수백 개의 식물과 나무가 자랄 수 있다   이 정원에서

⑩ One of the most famous green buildings / is in Milan, Italy. / It is called / Bosco
가장 유명한 녹색 건물 중 하나는   이탈리아의 밀라노에 있다   그것은 불린다   보스코

Verticale. / ⑪ Its name means "the vertical forest." /
베르티칼레라고   그것의 이름은 '수직의 숲'을 의미한다

본문 해석

대부분의 도시들은 붐빈다. 땅 위에 나무와 식물을 위한 공간이 거의 없다. 하지만 도시는 식물과 나무가 필요하다. 그것들은 공기를 깨끗하게 한다. 그것들은 또한 빗물을 흡수함으로써 홍수를 방지한다. 때때로 그것들은 동물들에게 서식지를 제공하고 사람들이 휴식하도록 돕는다. 그래서 도시의 사람들은 식물과 나무를 위한 새로운 장소를 찾았는데, 바로 머리 위 높은 곳이다. 건축가들은 현재 야외 정원이 있는 건물을 설계하고 있다. 수백 개의 식물과 나무가 이 정원에서 자랄 수 있다. 가장 유명한 녹색 건물 중 하나는 이탈리아의 밀라노에 있다. 그것은 보스코 베르티칼레라고 불린다. 그것의 이름은 '수직의 숲'을 의미한다.

구문 해설

② There is **little** space for trees and plants on the ground.
➜ little은 '거의 없는'의 의미이다. (*cf.* a little은 '조금'의 의미이다.)

⑤ They also prevent flooding **by absorbing** rain.

➡ 「by+v-ing」는 '~함으로써'의 의미로 〈방법〉을 나타낸다.

⑥ Sometimes, they **_provide_** homes **for** animals and _help_ people relax.

➡ 「provide A for B」는 'B에게 A를 제공하다'의 의미이다.

➡ 동사 provide와 help는 접속사 and로 병렬 연결되어 있다.

➡ 「help+목적어+동사원형[to-v]」은 '~가 …하는 것을 돕다'의 의미이다.

⑦ So people [in cities] have found a new place [for plants and trees]— high above their heads.

➡ 첫 번째 [ ]는 people을 수식하는 전치사구이고, 두 번째 [ ]는 a new place를 수식하는 전치사구이다.

⑨ Hundreds of plants and trees **can be grown** in these gardens.

➡ can be grown은 '자랄 수 있다'라는 의미로, 조동사와 함께 쓰인 수동태이다. 조동사 뒤에는 동사원형이 오므로, be동사의 원형인 be를 써서 「조동사+be+p.p.」로 나타낸다.

⑩ **One of the most famous green buildings is** in Milan, Italy.

➡ 「one of the+형용사의 최상급+복수 명사」는 '가장 ~한 …들 중 하나'의 의미로, 핵심 주어가 One이므로 동사는 단수형 동사 is가 왔다.

정답

1 audience **2** tag **3** fingerprint **4** flooding **5** theater **6** garden **7** ⓒ
8 ⓑ **9** ⓐ **10** ④ **11** ① **12** Hundreds of **13** register **14** These days
15 it's easy and painless to collect nose prints
16 Whistles don't cause accidents any more.
17 There is little space for trees and plants

문제 해설

1 audience: 청중, 관중

2 tag: 꼬리표

3 fingerprint: 지문

4 flooding: 홍수

5 theater: 극장

6 garden: 뜰, 정원

7 architect(건축가): ⓒ 건물을 설계하는 사람

8 loosen(느슨하게 하다): ⓑ 무언가를 덜 조이게 하다

9 painless(고통 없는, 아프지 않은): ⓐ 어떤 고통도 없는

10 우리는 공원에 <u>야외</u> 소풍을 갔다.
① 민감한 ② 좋은, 타당한 ③ 어리석은 ④ 실내의 ⑤ 독특한

11 질문이 있으면 손을 <u>들어</u>주세요.
① 내리다 ② 확인하다 ③ 다치게 하다 ④ 제거하다 ⑤ 모으다

12 hundreds of: 수백의

13 register: 등록하다

14 these days: 오늘날

15 가주어 it과 진주어 to collect nose prints를 이용하여 쓴다.

16 '더 이상 ~ 않다'라는 의미로, not ~ any more를 쓴다.

17 '거의 없는'이라는 의미로, little을 쓴다.

SECTION 06

1

정답 1 ③ 2 ④ 3 (1) T (2) T 4 ③

문제 해설

1 케이크에 초를 꽂는 생일 전통이 어떻게 시작되었는지 설명하는 글이므로, 주제로는 ③이 가장 알맞다.

2 '그러나 아마도 독일인들이 초를 꽂은 케이크를 생일 전통으로 만들었을 것이다'라는 내용의 주어진 문장은 고대 그리스의 최초의 케이크 초에 대한 내용과 1700년대에 아이들의 생일을 케이크로 축하하기 시작했다는 내용 사이인 ④에 오는 것이 가장 알맞다.

3 (1) 문장 ⑤를 통해 알 수 있다.

　　(2) 문장 ⑧을 통해 알 수 있다.

4 바로 뒤에 이어지는 문장 ⑪에서 아이들이 더 오래 살기를 바라는 부모의 바람을 나타낸다고 했다.

본문 직독 직해

① Cake with candles / is a fun birthday tradition. / ② But / how did it begin? / ③ Cake
초를 꽂은 케이크는　재미있는 생일 전통이다　그런데 그것이 어떻게 시작되었을까

with candles / dates back / to ancient Greece. / ④ The ancient Greeks / were probably
초를 꽂은 케이크는　거슬러 올라간다　고대 그리스로　고대 그리스인들이　아마도 최초의 사람들이었을

the first / to put candles on cake. / ⑤ They gave gifts / to Artemis, / the goddess of the
것이다　케이크에 초를 꽂은　그들은 선물을 바쳤다　아르테미스에게　달의 여신인

moon. / ⑥ They gave her / small cakes with candles. / ⑦ The candles made the cakes /
달의　그들은 그녀에게 바쳤다　초를 꽂은 작은 케이크를　초는 케이크를 만들었다

glow like the moon. / ⑧ Some people believed / that smoke from candles / carried
달처럼 빛나게　어떤 사람들은 믿었다　초에서 나온 연기가　기도를 실어

prayers / to heaven. /
나른다고　하늘로

However, / Germans probably made / cake with candles / a birthday tradition. /
그러나　독일인들이 아마도 만들었을 것이다　초를 꽂은 케이크를　생일 전통으로

⑨ In the 1700s / they started celebrating / children's birthdays / with cake. / ⑩ Parents
1700년대에　그들은 축하하기 시작했다　아이들의 생일을　케이크로　부모는

served a cake / with the same number of candles / as the child's age plus one. / ⑪ It
케이크를 내었다　같은 수의 초와 함께　아이의 나이에 하나를 더한 것과 (같은)　그것은

represented / the parents' hope / for their children / to live longer. /
나타냈다　부모의 바람을　그들의 아이들이　더 오래 살기를 (바라는)

본문 해석

　　초를 꽂은 케이크는 재미있는 생일 전통이다. 그런데 그것이 어떻게 시작되었을까? 초를 꽂은 케이크는 고대 그리스로 거슬러 올라간다. 아마도 고대 그리스인들이 케이크에 초를 꽂은 최초의 사람들이었을 것이다. 그들은 달의 여신인 아르테미스에게 선물을 바쳤다. 그들은 그녀에게 초를 꽂은 작은 케이크를 바쳤다. 초는 케이크를 달처럼 빛나게 만들었다. 어떤 사람들은 초에서 나온 연기가 기도를 하늘로 실어 나른다고 믿었다.

　　그러나 아마도 독일인들이 초를 꽂은 케이크를 생일 전통으로 만들었을 것이다. 1700년대에 그들은 케이크로 아이들의 생일을 축하하기 시작했다. 부모는 아이의 나이에 하나를 더한 것과 같은 수의 초를 꽂아 케이크를 내어 주었다. 그것은 아이들이 더 오래 살기를 바라는 부모의 바람을 나타냈다.

① **Cake** [with candles] **is** a fun birthday tradition.

　➡ 문장의 주어가 단수 명사인 Cake이므로 단수형 동사 is가 쓰였다.

　➡ [ ]는 Cake를 수식하는 전치사구이다.

④ The ancient Greeks were probably the first **to put** candles on cake.

　➡ to put은 '꽂은'의 의미로, 명사구 the first를 수식하는 형용사적 용법의 to부정사이다.

⑤ They gave gifts to **Artemis**, **the goddess of the moon**.

　➡ Artemis와 the goddess of the moon은 동격 관계로, 콤마(,)는 동격을 나타낸다.

⑥ They **gave her small cakes with candles**.

　➡ 「give A B」는 'A에게 B를 주다'의 의미로, her이 A, small cakes with candles가 B에 해당한다.

⑦ The candles **made the cakes glow** like the moon.

　➡ 「make+목적어+동사원형」은 '~을 …하게 만들다'의 의미이다.

⑧ Some people believed [**that** smoke from candles carried prayers to heaven].

　➡ that은 명사절을 이끄는 접속사로, [ ]는 동사 believed의 목적어 역할을 한다.

⑭ However, Germans probably **made cake with candles a birthday tradition**.

　➡ 「make A B」는 'A를 B로 만들다'의 의미로, 여기서는 cake with candles가 A, a birthday tradition
　　이 B에 해당한다.

⑨ In the 1700s they **started celebrating** children's birthdays with cake.

　➡ 「start+v-ing[to-v]」는 '~하기 시작하다'의 의미이다.

⑪ It represented the parents' hope **for their children** *to live* longer.

　➡ for their children은 to부정사(to live)의 의미상의 주어이다.

　➡ to live는 '살기 (바라는)'의 의미로, 명사구 the parents' hope를 수식하는 형용사적 용법의 to부정사구이다.

본책 • pp. 60-61

　1 ④　**2** ②　**3** (1) T (2) F　**4** burn, ice

1　화상을 입었을 때 얼음을 사용하는 방법이 실제로는 치료 효과가 없다는 내용의 글이므로, 주제로는 ④ '왜 화상
에 얼음을 대면 안 되는가'가 가장 알맞다.

　① 치료를 위한 얼음의 사용　　　　　　② 통증을 가라앉히는 단순한 방법들

　③ 피부를 관리하는 방법　　　　　　　⑤ 왜 주방에서 조심해야 하는가

2　주어진 문장은 '그들은 얼음이 실제로는 화상을 더 느리게 낫도록 한다는 것을 발견했다'는 내용이므로, 과학자들
　이 치료법의 치료 효과를 비교했다는 내용의 문장 ⑤와 화상에 얼음을 사용하는 것의 또 다른 영향을 설명하는
　문장 ⑥ 사이인 ②에 오는 것이 가장 자연스럽다.

3　(1) 문장 ⑥에 언급되어 있다.

　(2) 문장 ⑫에서 피부가 2주가 지나도 낫지 않을 경우에 진찰을 받으라고 했다.

4　문장 ④-⑥에 언급되어 있다.

> 화상을 입으면, 그 위에 얼음을 대면 안 된다. 대신 그곳을 시원한 흐르는 물 아래에 두어라.

① In the kitchen, / you burn your hand / on a hot pan. / ② You run / to get some
주방에서　　　　　당신은 손을 덴다　　　　뜨거운 팬에　　　　당신은 뛴다　얼음을 가지러
ice / to ease the pain. / ③ Stop! / ④ Ice doesn't help. /
통증을 가라앉힐　　　　멈춰라　　얼음은 도움이 되지 않는다
⑤ Some scientists compared / the treatment effects / of ice and other cures. / They
몇몇 과학자들이 비교했다　　　　치료 효과를　　　　얼음과 다른 치료법의　　　그들은
found / ice actually made the burn / get better more slowly. / ⑥ Also, / ice caused /
발견했다　얼음이 실제로는 화상을 만들었다는 것을　더 느리게 낫도록　　게다가　얼음은 야기했다
frostbite and the most serious skin damage. /
동상과 가장 심각한 피부 손상을
⑦ So, / how can we treat a burn? / ⑧ Put the burn / under cool, running water / for
그렇다면 우리는 어떻게 화상을 치료할 수 있을까　화상을 두어라　　시원한 흐르는 물 아래에
20 minutes. / ⑨ Or / you can use a cool, wet cloth. / ⑩ Then / clean the area. / ⑪ In
20분간　　　　또는　시원한 젖은 헝겊을 사용해도 된다　　　그런 다음　그 부위를 깨끗하게 해라
this way, / you can treat most minor burns / at home. / ⑫ However, / see a doctor / if
이 방법으로　당신은 대부분의 가벼운 화상을 치료할 수 있다　집에서　　그러나　　진찰을 받아라
your skin doesn't get better / in two weeks. /
피부가 낫지 않으면　　　　　2주 후에

당신은 주방에서 뜨거운 팬에 손을 덴다. 당신은 통증을 가라앉힐 얼음을 가지러 뛴다. 멈춰라! 얼음은 도움이
되지 않는다.

몇몇 과학자들이 얼음과 다른 치료법의 치료 효과를 비교했다. 그들은 얼음이 실제로는 화상을 더 느리게 낫도
록 한다는 것을 발견했다. 게다가, 얼음은 동상과 가장 심각한 피부 손상을 야기했다.

그렇다면, 우리는 어떻게 화상을 치료할 수 있을까? 화상 입은 곳을 시원한 흐르는 물 아래에 20분간 두어라.
또는 시원한 젖은 헝겊을 사용해도 된다. 그런 다음 그 부위를 깨끗하게 해라. 이 방법으로, 대부분의 가벼운 화상
을 집에서 치료할 수 있다. 그러나 피부가 2주가 지나도록 낫지 않으면 진찰을 받아라.

② You run **to get** some ice *to ease* the pain.
  ➡ to get은 '가져오기 위해'의 의미로, 〈목적〉을 나타내는 부사적 용법의 to부정사이다.
  ➡ to ease는 '가라앉힐'의 의미로, some ice를 수식하는 형용사적 용법의 to부정사이다.
⑤ Some scientists compared the treatment effects **of ice** and **other cures**.
  ➡ 전치사 of의 목적어 ice와 other cures가 접속사 and로 연결되어 있다.
⑤ They found [(**that**) ice actually *made the burn get* better more slowly].
  ➡ [ ]는 동사 found의 목적어 역할을 하는 명사절로, 접속사 that이 생략되었다.
  ➡ 「make+목적어+동사원형」은 '~가 …하게 하다'의 의미이다.
⑫ However, see a doctor **if** your skin doesn't get better *in* two weeks.
  ➡ if는 '만약 ~라면'의 의미로, 〈조건〉을 나타내는 접속사이다.
  ➡ in은 '~ 후에, ~ 지나'의 의미로 〈시간의 경과〉를 나타내는 전치사이다.

3

정답 **1** ③ **2** ③ **3** 그림에 죽은 고래가 숨겨져 있었다는 것 **4** ④

문제 해설

1 17세기의 한 그림을 복원하는 중에 그림 속에 죽은 고래 한 마리가 숨겨져 있었다는 것을 발견했다는 내용의 글이므로, 주제로는 ③이 가장 알맞다.

2 ③: 문장 ③에서 해변에 사람들이 있는 장면을 묘사한 그림이라고는 했으나 해변에서 그려진 그림이라는 언급은 없다.

①은 문장 ①에, ②는 문장 ②에, ④는 문장 ⑤-⑥에, ⑤는 문장 ⑪에 언급되어 있다.

3 문장 ⑨를 통해 알 수 있다.

4 앞 문장에서 죽은 고래가 불쾌한 대상으로 여겨졌다고 했으므로, 빈칸에는 ④ '불운'이 가장 알맞다.

① 평화   ② 힘   ③ 승리   ④ 장수

본문 직독 직해

① One restorer was cleaning / a 17th-century painting. / ② It was made / by Dutch
한 복원 전문가가 닦고 있었다　　　17세기 그림 하나를　　　　　그것은 만들어졌다[그려졌다]

painter Hendrick van Anthonissen. / ③ The painting was a scene / of people on a
네덜란드 화가 핸드릭 반 안소나이젠에 의해　　　그 그림은 장면이었다　　　해변에 사람들이 있는

beach. / ④ But / it had a secret. / ⑤ As she cleaned the painting, / a thin layer of paint /
해변에　　그런데　그것은 비밀을 갖고 있었다　그녀가 그림을 닦았을 때　　　얇은 물감 한 겹이

came off. / ⑥ She saw something strange. / ⑦ Surprisingly, / it was a huge fin! / ⑧ She
떼어졌다　　　그녀는 이상한 무언가를 보았다　　　놀랍게도　　그것은 거대한 지느러미였다　그녀는

continued to remove / the layers of paint. / ⑨ Soon / a dead whale appeared / on the
계속해서 제거했다　　　물감의 겹들을　　　곧　　죽은 고래 한 마리가 나타났다

beach. /
해변에

⑩ But / why was the whale hidden? / ⑪ Researchers said / dead whales were / an
그런데　고래는 왜 숨겨졌을까　　　　연구가들은 말했다　　죽은 고래는 ~이었다고

unpleasant subject / for the people of that time. / ⑫ Some people believed / they meant
불쾌한 대상　　　　그 당시의 사람들에게　　　어떤 사람들은 믿었다　　　그것들이 불운을

bad luck. / ⑬ So / it is likely that / the whale was covered up. / ⑭ But / that's just one
의미한다고　　그래서　가능성이 있다　　고래가 완전히 가려졌을　　　그러나　그것은 그저 하나의

guess. / ⑮ We may never know! /
추측일 뿐이다　우리는 결코 알지 못할지도 모른다

본문 해석

　한 복원 전문가가 17세기 그림 한 점을 닦고 있었다. 그것은 네덜란드 화가 핸드릭 반 안소나이젠에 의해 그려졌다. 그 그림은 해변에 사람들이 있는 장면이었다. 그런데 그것은 비밀을 갖고 있었다. 그녀가 그림을 닦았을 때, 얇은 물감 한 겹이 떼어졌다. 그녀는 이상한 무언가를 보았다. 놀랍게도, 그것은 거대한 지느러미였다! 그녀는 물감의 겹들을 계속해서 제거했다. 곧 해변에 죽은 고래 한 마리가 나타났다.

　그런데 고래는 왜 숨겨졌을까? 연구가들은 그 당시의 사람들에게 죽은 고래가 불쾌한 대상이었다고 말했다. 어떤 사람들은 그것들이 <u>불운</u>을 의미한다고 믿었다. 그래서 고래가 완전히 가려졌을 가능성이 있다. 그러나 그것은 그저 하나의 추측일 뿐이다. 우리는 결코 알지 못할지도 모른다!

① One restorer **was cleaning** a 17th-century painting.

→ was cleaning은 '닦고 있었다'의 의미로, 「be동사의 과거형+v-ing」의 과거진행형이다.

② It **was made** by Dutch painter Hendrick van Anthonissen.

→ was made는 '만들어졌다'의 의미로, 「be+p.p.」의 수동태이다.

⑤ **As** she cleaned the painting, a thin layer of paint came off.

→ As는 '~할 때'의 의미로, 〈때〉를 나타내는 접속사로 쓰였다.

⑥ She saw **something strange**.

→ -thing으로 끝나는 대명사는 형용사가 뒤에서 수식하므로, 형용사 strange가 something 뒤에 왔다.

⑧ She **continued to remove** the layers of paint.

→ 「continue+to-v[v-ing]」는 '계속해서 ~하다'의 의미이다.

⑪ Researchers said [(**that**) dead whales were an unpleasant subject for the people {of that time}].

→ [ ]는 동사 said의 목적어 역할을 하는 명사절로, 접속사 that이 생략되었다.

→ { }는 the people을 수식하는 전치사구이다.

⑬ So **it is likely that** the whale was covered up.

→ 「it is likely that ~」은 '~일 것 같다, ~일 가능성이 있다'의 의미이다.

정답　**1** candle　**2** whale　**3** pan　**4** cloth　**5** smoke　**6** hide　**7** ⓑ　**8** ⓒ　**9** ⓐ
10 ②　**11** ①　**12** get better　**13** dates back to　**14** come off
15 She continued to remove the layers of paint.
16 It represented the parent's hope for their children to live longer.
17 Some scientists compared the treatment effects of ice and other cures.

**문제
해설**

1　candle: 초, 양초

2　whale: 고래

3　pan: (손잡이가 있는) 냄비, 팬

4　cloth: 천, 옷감

5　smoke: 연기

6　hide: 감추다, 숨기다

7　carry(나르다): ⓑ 무언가를 한 곳에서 다른 곳으로 옮기다

8　ease((고통 등을) 덜어 주다): ⓒ 무언가를 더 낫거나 덜 고통스럽게 만들다

9　dead(죽은): ⓐ 더 이상 살아있지 않은

10　그 부상은 매우 <u>심각해</u> 보였다.
　　① 나쁜　② 작은, 가벼운　③ 비슷한　④ 가능성 있는　⑤ 중요한

11　이 방에서는 <u>불쾌한</u> 냄새가 난다.
　　① 좋은　② 냄새가 나는　③ 이상한　④ 독특한　⑤ 익숙한

12　get better: 낫다, 호전되다

13　date back to: ~까지 거슬러 올라가다

14　come off: 떼어지다, 떨어지다

15　'계속해서 ~하다'라는 의미의 「continue+to-v」를 쓴다.

16　'(그들의) 아이들이'라는 의미로, 「for+명사」 형태의 to부정사의 의미상의 주어를 쓴다. 이어서 '살기 (바라는)'
　　의 의미로, 명사구 the parent's hope를 수식하는 형용사적 용법의 to부정사구를 to live longer을 쓴다.

17　'A와 B를 비교하다'라는 의미로, compare A and B를 쓴다.

SECTION 07

1

정답 1 ⑤ 2 ⑤ 3 ①, ③, ⑤ 4 awake, asleep

문제 해설

1 비행기 이착륙 시 잠을 자면 귀 내부의 압력을 조절하기 위한 행동을 할 수 없어서 귀에 손상을 줄 수 있다는 내용의 글이므로, 주제로는 ⑤가 가장 알맞다.

2 이착륙 시에 잠을 자면 귀가 손상될 수 있다는 내용 중에, 시끄러운 음악을 듣는 것이 청력 상실로 이어질 수 있다는 내용의 (e)는 글의 흐름과 무관하다.

3 ①, ③은 문장 ⑦에, ⑤는 문장 ⑧에 언급되어 있다.

4 문장 ⑨, ⑭에 언급되어 있다.

> 이륙과 착륙 동안 <u>깨어</u> 있어야 한다. <u>잠들어</u> 있을 때는 귀 내부의 압력을 낮추기 위한 어떤 것도 할 수가 없다.

본문 직독 직해

① You get on a flight / and put on your seat belt. / ② You want to get some sleep. /
당신은 비행기에 탑승한다   그리고 안전띠를 맨다   당신은 잠을 좀 자고 싶다

③ But / sleeping / during takeoff and landing / is not a good idea. / ④ At these times, /
그러나 잠을 자는 것은 이륙과 착륙 동안에   좋은 생각이 아니다   이때는

the air pressure in the airplane / changes quickly. / ⑤ This changes the pressure / in your
비행기 안의 기압이   빠르게 변한다   이는 압력을 변화시킨다   당신

ears. / ⑥ Your ears may pop. / ⑦ To reduce the pressure / in your ears, / you can yawn or
귀 내부의   당신의 귀가 먹먹해질지도 모른다   압력을 낮추기 위해   귀 내부의   당신은 하품을 하거나

swallow. / ⑧ Chewing gum helps, / too. / ⑨ But / you cannot do these things / when
침을 삼킬 수 있다   껌을 씹는 것이 도움이 된다   또한   하지만 당신은 이런 것들을 할 수 없다

you are asleep. / ⑩ This could damage your ears. / ⑪ You might feel dizzy. / ⑫ At worst /
당신이 자고 있을 때는   이것이 귀에 손상을 줄 수 있다   당신은 어지러울지도 모른다   최악의 경우에

you could lose / some of your hearing. / (⑬ Listening to loud music / might lead to
당신은 잃을 수도 있다   청력 일부를   시끄러운 음악을 듣는 것은   청력 상실로 이어질

hearing loss. /)
수도 있다

⑭ So / next time you feel sleepy / on an airplane, / remember: / be awake / during
그러니 다음에 당신이 졸음이 오면   비행기에서   기억하라   깨어 있어라

takeoff and landing. /
이륙과 착륙 동안에는

본문 해석

　당신은 비행기에 탑승해서 안전띠를 맨다. 당신은 잠을 좀 자고 싶다. 그러나 이륙과 착륙 동안에 자는 것은 좋은 생각이 아니다. 이때는, 기내 기압이 빠르게 변한다. 이는 귀 내부의 압력을 변화시킨다. 당신의 귀가 먹먹해질지도 모른다. 귀 내부의 압력을 낮추기 위해 당신은 하품을 하거나 침을 삼킬 수 있다. 껌을 씹는 것도 도움이 된다. 하지만 당신이 자고 있을 때는 이런 것들을 할 수 없다. 이것이 귀에 손상을 줄 수 있다. 당신은 어지러울지도 모른다. 최악의 경우에 당신은 청력 일부를 잃을 수도 있다. (시끄러운 음악을 듣는 것은 청력 상실로 이어질 수도 있다.)
　그러니 다음에 비행기에서 졸음이 오면, 기억하라. 이륙과 착륙 동안에는 깨어 있어라.

② You **want to get** some sleep.

→ 「want+to-v」는 '~하기를 원하다, ~하고 싶어 하다'의 의미이다.

③ But [**sleeping** *during* takeoff and landing] **is** not a good idea.

→ [ ]는 주어 역할을 하는 동명사구이며, 동명사구는 단수 취급하므로 단수형 동사 is가 쓰였다.

→ during은 '~ 동안'의 의미인 전치사이다.

④ At **these times**, *the air pressure* [in the airplane] *changes* quickly.

→ these times는 앞 문장의 takeoff and landing을 가리킨다.

→ 전치사구 [ ]의 수식을 받는 the air pressure가 주어, changes가 동사이다.

⑦ **To reduce** the pressure in your ears, you can yawn or swallow.

→ To reduce는 '낮추기 위해'의 의미로, 〈목적〉을 나타내는 부사적 용법의 to부정사이다.

⑪ You might **feel dizzy**.

→ 「feel+형용사」는 '~하게 느끼다'의 의미이다.

⑬ [Listening to loud music] might **lead to** hearing loss.

→ [ ]는 주어 역할을 하는 동명사구이다.

→ lead to는 '~로 이어지다'의 의미이다.

⑭ So **next time** you feel sleepy on an airplane, remember: be awake during takeoff and landing.

→ 「next time ~」은 '다음에 ~할 때[하면]'의 의미인 접속사이다.

본책 ● pp. 70-71

정답 **1** ③   **2** ⓐ: whistles ⓑ: referees   **3** ②   **4** (1) T (2) F

**문제
해설**

1 스포츠에서 심판이 호루라기를 사용하게 된 과정을 설명하는 글이므로, 제목으로는 ③ '스포츠에서의 호루라기 사용'이 가장 알맞다.

① 호루라기는 언제 사용되는가?　　　　② 심판: 스포츠 경찰

④ 경찰을 위한 유용한 발명품들　　　　⑤ 경기장에서의 군중 관련 문제

2 ⓐ: 심판들이 항상 호루라기를 가지고 있었던 것은 아니라는 내용으로, them은 앞 문장의 whistles를 가리킨다.

ⓑ: 앞 문장에서 심판들이 무언가가 필요했다고 했고, 한 발명가가 그들에게 해결책을 주었다는 내용으로, them은 앞 문장의 referees를 가리킨다.

3 '그러나 19세기에 스포츠가 인기를 얻게 되었다'는 내용의 주어진 문장은 소리치는 것이 소규모 경기에서는 괜찮았다는 내용의 문장 ④와 군중이 더 많아지고 시끄러워졌다는 내용의 문장 ⑤ 사이인 ②에 오는 것이 가장 알맞다.

4 (1) 문장 ⑧-⑩을 통해 알 수 있다.

(2) 문장 ⑩에서 Joseph Hudson이 호루라기를 스포츠에 도입했다고 했다.

① Whistles are useful / for referees. / ② But / they didn't always have them. / ③ At
호루라기는 유용하다   심판에게   그러나 그들이 항상 그것들을 가지고 있었던 것은 아니다

first, / they waved flags and shouted / to get players' attention. / ④ Shouting was fine /
처음에는 그들은 깃발을 흔들고 소리쳤다   선수들의 주의를 끌기 위해   소리치는 것은 괜찮았다

for small games. / But / in the 19th century, / sports became popular. / ⑤ The crowds
소규모 경기에서는   그러나 19세기에   스포츠가 인기를 얻게 되었다   군중이 ~해졌다

became / bigger and louder. / ⑥ In the noise, / players couldn't hear the referees. /
더 많고 더 시끄럽게   소음 속에서   선수들은 심판의 소리를 들을 수가 없었다

⑦ Referees really needed something! /
심판은 정말 무언가가 필요했다

⑧ Inventor Joseph Hudson / gave them a solution. / ⑨ He invented a new whistle / in
발명가 Joseph Hudson이   그들에게 해결책을 주었다   그는 새로운 호루라기를 발명했다

the 1880s. / ⑩ It was for the police / at first, / but later / he introduced it / to sports. /
1880년대에   그것은 경찰을 위한 것이었다 처음에는 하지만 이후에 그가 그것을 도입했다   스포츠에

⑪ It could be heard / in large crowds. / ⑫ It was much better / than shouting! / ⑬ Soon, /
그것은 들릴 수 있었다   수많은 군중 속에서   그것은 훨씬 더 좋았다   소리치는 것보다   곧

the whistle became common. /
호루라기가 흔해졌다

⑭ Now / whistles are used / in most noisy sports, / and even in the Olympics. /
현재   호루라기는 사용된다   대부분의 시끌벅적한 스포츠에서   그리고 심지어 올림픽에서도

심판에게 호루라기는 유용하다. 그러나 그들이 항상 호루라기를 가지고 있지는 않았다. 처음에는, 그들은 선수들의 주의를 끌기 위해 깃발을 흔들고 소리쳤다. 소리치는 것은 소규모 경기에서는 괜찮았다. 그러나 19세기에 스포츠가 인기를 얻게 되었다. 군중이 더 많아지고 더 시끄러워졌다. 소음 속에서 선수들은 심판의 소리를 들을 수가 없었다. 심판은 정말 무언가가 필요했다!

발명가 Joseph Hudson이 그들에게 해결책을 주었다. 그는 1880년대에 새로운 호루라기를 발명했다. 그것은 처음에는 경찰을 위한 것이었지만, 이후에 그가 그것을 스포츠에 도입했다. 그것은 수많은 군중 속에서 들릴 수 있었다. 그것은 소리치는 것보다 훨씬 더 좋았다! 곧, 호루라기가 흔해졌다.

현재 호루라기는 대부분의 시끌벅적한 스포츠에서, 그리고 심지어 올림픽에서도 사용된다.

② But they did**n't always** have them.
→ 「not always」는 '항상 ~인 것은 아니다'의 의미이다.

④ **Shouting was** fine for small games.
→ Shouting은 주어 역할을 하는 동명사이며, 동명사는 단수 취급하므로 단수형 동사 was가 쓰였다.

⑤ The crowds **became bigger** and **louder**.
→ 「become+형용사의 비교급」은 '더 ~해지다, 더 ~하게 되다'의 의미로, 여기서는 형용사의 비교급 bigger와 louder가 접속사 and로 병렬 연결되어 있다.

⑧ Inventor Joseph Hudson **gave them a solution**.
→ 「give A B」는 'A에게 B를 주다'의 의미로, them이 A, a solution이 B에 해당한다.

⑫ It was **much** better than shouting!
→ much는 '더욱, 훨씬'의 의미로, 비교급을 강조하는 표현이다. even, still, a lot, far도 비교급을 강조할 때 쓸 수 있다.

정답 **1** ③　　**2** (1) F (2) T　　**3** (고릴라들은) 더 크게 노래한다.　　**4** eat, happy

문제 해설

1 고릴라가 맛있는 음식을 먹으면 행복을 느끼고 노래를 한다는 내용의 글이므로, 제목으로는 ③ '맛있는 음식이 고릴라를 노래하게 만든다!'가 가장 알맞다.

① 고릴라는 노래를 할 수 있는가?　　　　　　② 고릴라도 감정이 있는가?

④ Eva Luef: 역사상 최고의 동물학자　　　　⑤ 인간과 고릴라의 차이점

2 (1) 문장 ③에서 콩고의 야생 고릴라를 연구했다고 했다.

(2) 문장 ⑧-⑨에 언급되어 있다.

3 문장 ⑫에 언급되어 있다.

> Q: 고릴라들은 그들이 매우 좋아하는 음식을 먹을 때 무엇을 하는가?

4 | 보기 |　행복한　　　잠자다　　　먹다　　　배고픈

> 고릴라들은 먹을 때 두 가지 소리를 낸다. 이 소리는 그들이 행복하다는 것을 보여 준다.

본문 직독 직해

① We feel happy / when we eat delicious food. / ② Gorillas do too, / and they show
우리는 행복을 느낀다　우리가 맛있는 음식을 먹을 때　　　고릴라도 그렇다　　　그리고 그들은

it! /
그것을 보여 준다

③ Zoologist Eva Luef studied / wild gorillas / in the Congo. / ④ She found / that they
동물학자 Eva Luef는 연구했다　　　야생 고릴라를　　콩고에 있는　　　　　그녀는 발견했다　그들이

made two different sounds / during meals. / ⑤ One sound was a deep, steady
두 가지 다른 소리를 낸다는 것을　　　식사 중에　　　한 가지 소리는 낮고 고정적인 콧노래였다

humming. / ⑥ It sounded / like a sigh of satisfaction. / ⑦ The other sound was like a
그것은 들렸다　만족의 한숨처럼　　　　다른 소리는 노래 같았다

song. / ⑧ Gorillas sang different notes / to make their own melody. / ⑨ Each gorilla has /
고릴라들은 각기 다른 음을 노래했다　　자신만의 멜로디를 만들기 위해　　　고릴라 각자는 갖고 있다

its own style. / ⑩ You can tell / who is singing. / ⑪ Their songs might tell others / to come
자신만의 스타일을　당신은 구분할 수 있다　누가 노래하고 있는지　그들의 노래는 다른 이들에게 말하는 것일지도 모른다

and enjoy the food / with them. / ⑫ When they have their favorite food, / they sing more
와서 음식을 즐기자고　　　그들과 같이　　　그들이 매우 좋아하는 음식을 먹을 때　　　그들은 더 크게

loudly! / ⑬ These two habits are ways / to show / their happiness. /
노래한다　이 두 가지 습관은 방법이다　보여 주는　그들의 행복을

본문 해석

우리는 맛있는 음식을 먹을 때 행복을 느낀다. 고릴라도 그러한데, 그들은 그것을 보여 준다!

동물학자 Eva Luef는 콩고에 있는 야생 고릴라를 연구했다. 그녀는 그들이 식사 중에 두 가지 다른 소리를 낸다는 것을 발견했다. 한 가지 소리는 낮고 고정적인 콧노래였다. 그것은 만족의 한숨처럼 들렸다. 다른 소리는 노래 같았다. 고릴라들은 자신만의 멜로디를 만들기 위해 각기 다른 음을 노래했다. 고릴라 각자는 자신만의 스타일을 가지고 있다. 당신은 누가 노래하고 있는지 구분할 수 있다. 그들의 노래는 다른 이들에게 와서 음식을 그들과 같이 즐기자고 말하는 것일지도 모른다. 그들이 매우 좋아하는 음식을 먹을 때는, 더 크게 노래한다! 이 두 가지 습관은 그들의 행복을 보여 주는 방법이다.

① We **feel happy** *when* we eat delicious food.
  → 「feel+형용사」는 '~하게 느끼다'의 의미이다.
  → when은 '~할 때'의 의미로, 〈때〉를 나타내는 접속사이다.
② Gorillas **do** too, and they show *it*!
  → do는 feel happy when they eat delicious food를 대신한다.
  → it은 앞 절의 내용을 가리킨다.
④ She found [that they made two different sounds **during** meals].
  → [ ]는 동사 found의 목적어 역할을 하는 명사절이다.
  → during은 '~ 동안, ~(하는) 중에'의 의미인 전치사이다.
⑥ It **sounded like** a sigh of satisfaction.
  → 「sound like+명사」는 '~처럼 들리다'의 의미이다.
⑧ Gorillas sang different notes **to make** their own melody.
  → to make는 '만들기 위해'의 의미로, 〈목적〉을 나타내는 부사적 용법의 to부정사이다.
⑨ **Each gorilla has** its own style.
  → 「each+단수 명사」는 '각각의 ~'의 의미로, 단수 취급하므로 단수형 동사 has가 쓰였다.
⑩ You can tell [who is singing].
  → [ ]는 tell의 목적어 역할을 하는 간접의문문이다.
⑪ Their songs might **tell** others **to come** and (**to**) **enjoy** the food with them.
  → 「tell+목적어+to-v」는 '~에게 …하라고 말하다'의 의미이다.
  → to come과 (to) enjoy는 접속사 and로 병렬 연결되어 있다.
⑬ These two habits are ways **to show** their happiness.
  → to show는 '보여 주는'의 의미로, 명사 ways를 수식하는 형용사적 용법의 to부정사이다.

정답
1 yawn　**2** stadium　**3** flight　**4** sigh　**5** whistle　**6** meal　**7** ⓒ　**8** ⓐ　**9** ⓑ
10 ③　**11** ①　**12** put on　**13** not always　**14** sounds like
15 The crowds became bigger and louder.
16 You can tell who is singing.
17 Listening to loud music might lead to hearing loss.

문제 해설

1 yawn: 하품하다

2 stadium: 경기장

3 flight: 비행; 항공기

4 sigh: 한숨, 탄식

5 whistle: 호각, 호루라기

6 meal: 식사

7 crowd(사람들, 군중): ⓒ 같은 장소에 있는 많은 수의 사람들

8 invent(발명하다): ⓐ 새로운 무언가를 만들다

9 steady(고정적인, 한결같은): ⓑ 시간이 지나도 변하지 않는

10 ┌ 이륙 시에 휴대폰을 꺼 주십시오. ┐
　　① 여행　② 비행　③ 착륙　④ 경기장　⑤ 콧노래

11 ┌ 그 교실은 쉬는 시간 동안 시끄러웠다. ┐
　　① 조용한　② 흔한　③ 인기 있는　④ 유용한　⑤ 야생의

12 put on: ~을 입다, 착용하다

13 not always: 항상 ~인 것은 아니다

14 sound like: ~처럼 들리다

15 '더 ~해지다'라는 의미의 「become+형용사의 비교급」을 쓴다.

16 문장의 동사 tell의 목적어로 '누가 ~하는지'라는 의미의 간접의문문을 쓴다.

17 '듣는 것'이라는 의미로, 주어 역할을 하는 동명사 listening을 쓴다. '~로 이어지다'라는 의미는 lead to를 쓴다.

SECTION 08

1

정답 1 ③   2 ②   3 ⑤   4 candles, letter

문제 해설

1 노르웨이의 크리스마스 마을인 드뢰박을 소개하는 글이므로, 제목으로는 ③ '노르웨이의 크리스마스 마을'이 가장 알맞다.

① 산타클로스는 누구인가?   ② 크리스마스의 기원
④ 산타에게 크리스마스카드를 써라!   ⑤ 세계의 크리스마스 전통

2 Tregaarden's Julehus에 관한 내용 뒤에, 그 옆집에 산타의 우체국이 있다는 내용의 (A), 우표를 사서 산타에게 편지를 보낼 수 있다는 내용의 (C), 그가 편지를 11월과 12월에 읽을 것이라는 내용의 (B)로 이어지는 흐름이 가장 알맞다.

3 ⑤: 문장 ⑬에서 운이 좋으면 크리스마스에 산타와 함께 사진을 찍을 수 있다고 했다.
①은 문장 ④에, ②는 문장 ⑤-⑥에, ③은 문장 ⑨에, ④는 문장 ⑩에 언급되어 있다.

4 문장 ⑧과 ⑩-⑫에 언급되어 있다.

> Tregaarden's Julehus에서 크리스마스 장식과 양초를 살 수 있으며, 산타의 우체국에서 산타에게 편지를 보낼 수 있다.

본문 직독 직해

① Do you love Christmas? / ② Then / you'll love Drøbak, Norway. / ③ It's
당신은 크리스마스를 매우 좋아하는가   그렇다면   당신은 노르웨이의 드뢰박을 아주 좋아할 것이다

Christmas / all year / in Drøbak! / ④ In Norway, / people say / that Santa Claus was
크리스마스이다   일 년 내내   드뢰박에서는   노르웨이에서   사람들은 말한다   산타클로스가 태어났다고

born / in Drøbak. / ⑤ You can see special street signs / about Santa / there. / ⑥ They
드뢰박에서   당신은 특별한 거리 표지판을 볼 수 있다   산타에 관한   그곳에서   그것들은

tell you / to watch out for Santa. /
당신에게 말한다 산타를 조심하라고

⑦ The village is mainly famous / for Tregaarden's Julehus, or "Christmas House." /
마을은 주로 유명하다   Tregaarden's Julehus, 즉 '크리스마스 집'으로

⑧ You can buy / Christmas decorations and candles / there. / ⑨ Around 250,000 people
당신은 살 수 있다   크리스마스 장식품과 양초를   그곳에서   약 25만 명의 사람들이 그곳을

visit it / each year. / ⑩ And Santa's post office is next door. / ⑫ You can buy stamps /
방문한다   매년   그리고 산타의 우체국이 옆집에 있다   당신은 우표를 살 수 있다

and send Santa a letter. / ⑪ He will read your letter / during November and December. /
그리고 산타에게 편지를 보낼 수 있다   그는 당신의 편지를 읽을 것이다   11월과 12월 동안

⑬ If you're lucky, / you can take a picture / with him / on Christmas Day! /
당신이 운이 좋다면   당신은 사진을 찍을 수 있다   그와 함께   크리스마스에

본문 해석

당신은 크리스마스를 매우 좋아하는가? 그렇다면 노르웨이의 드뢰박을 아주 좋아할 것이다. 드뢰박에서는 일 년 내내 크리스마스이다! 노르웨이에서 사람들은 산타클로스가 드뢰박에서 태어났다고 말한다. 그곳에서 산타에 관한 특별한 거리 표지판을 볼 수 있다. 그것들은 당신에게 산타를 조심하라고 말해 준다.

마을은 주로 Tregaarden's Julehus, 즉 '크리스마스 집'으로 유명하다. 그곳에서 크리스마스 장식품과 양초를 살 수 있다. 매년 약 25만 명의 사람들이 그곳을 방문한다. (A) 그리고 산타의 우체국이 옆집에 있다. (C) 당신은 우표를 사서 산타에게 편지를 보낼 수 있다. (B) 그는 당신의 편지를 11월과 12월 동안 읽을 것이다. 당신이 운이 좋다면, 크리스마스에 산타와 함께 사진을 찍을 수 있다!

④ In Norway, people say [that Santa Claus **was born** in Drøbak].
→ [ ]는 동사 say의 목적어 역할을 하는 명사절이다.
→ was born은 '태어났다'의 의미로, 「be+p.p.」의 수동태이다.

⑥ They **tell you to watch out** for Santa.
→ 「tell+목적어+to-v」는 '~에게 …하라고 말하다'의 의미이다.

⑫ You can **buy** stamps and **send** Santa a letter.
→ 조동사 can 뒤에 동사원형 buy와 send가 접속사 and로 병렬 연결되어 있다.
→ 「send A B」는 'A에게 B를 보내다'의 의미로, Santa가 A, a letter가 B에 해당한다.

⑬ **If** you're lucky, you can take a picture with him on Christmas Day!
→ If는 '만약 ~라면'의 의미로, 〈조건〉을 나타내는 접속사이다.

본책 • pp. 80-81

2

정답 **1** ③   **2** (1) F (2) T   **3** 소화 문제를 일으킬 수 있기 때문에   **4** swallow, digest

**문제
해설**

1 껌을 삼켰을 때 몸속에서 일어나는 일을 설명하는 글이므로, 주제로는 ③이 가장 알맞다.

2 (1) 문장 ⑥에서 우리 몸은 껌을 여느 다른 음식과 똑같이 취급한다고 했다.
(2) 문장 ⑨-⑩에 언급되어 있다.

3 문장 ⑭에 언급되어 있다.

4

| 보기 | 삼키다 | 소화시키다 | 야기하다 | 머무르다, 남다 |

> 껌을 <u>삼키면</u>, 몸은 그것으로부터 영양분을 저장한다. 그러나 위는 껌 기초제를 <u>소화시키지</u> 못한다. 그래서 몸은 단순히 그것을 밀어낸다.

**본문
직독
직해**

① You accidentally swallowed gum. / ② Oops! / ③ According to some people, / now /
　당신은 잘못해서 껌을 삼켰다　　　　　이런　　　몇몇 사람들에 따르면　　　　이제

it will stay / in your body / for seven years. / ④ Is that true? /
그것은 머물 것이다　당신의 몸속에　7년 동안　　　　　　그게 사실일까

⑤ No! / ⑥ Your body treats gum / like any other food. / ⑦ First, / some parts of it /
　아니다　　당신의 몸은 껌을 취급한다　여느 다른 음식과 똑같이　　우선　　그것의 일부는

break down / in your stomach. / ⑧ Then / your body saves any nutrients. / ⑨ But / your
분해된다　　　당신의 위에서　　　　그런 다음　당신의 몸은 어떤 영양소든 저장한다　　그러나

body cannot digest one part: / the gum base. / ⑩ The chemicals in the gum base / don't
몸이 한 부분은 소화시키지 못한다　껌 기초제이다　　　껌 기초제 속의 화학 물질은

본문 해석

당신은 잘못해서 껌을 삼켰다. 이런! 몇몇 사람들에 따르면, 이제 그것은 7년 동안 당신의 몸속에 머물 것이다. 그게 사실일까?

아니다! 당신의 몸은 껌을 여느 다른 음식과 똑같이 취급한다. 우선, 그것의 일부는 당신의 위에서 분해된다. 그런 다음 당신의 몸은 어떤 영양소든 저장한다. 그러나 몸이 한 부분은 소화시키지 못하는데, 바로 껌 기초제이다. 껌 기초제 속의 화학 물질은 쉽게 분해되지 않는다. 그래서 몸은 단순히 그것을 소화 기관을 통해 밀어낸다. 그리고 그것은 마침내 몸을 떠난다.

껌을 삼키는 것은 대개는 무해하지만, 그것을 습관으로 만들지는 마라. 한꺼번에 너무 많은 껌을 삼키는 것은 소화 문제를 일으킬 수 있다!

구문 해설

⑥ Your body treats gum **like** any other food.
→ like는 '~와 마찬가지로, ~와 (똑)같이'의 의미인 전치사로 쓰였다.

⑦ First, **some parts** [of it] **break** down in your stomach.
→ [ ]는 some parts를 수식하는 전치사구이다.
→ 문장의 주어가 some parts로 복수 명사이므로, 복수형 동사 break가 쓰였다.

⑩ **The chemicals** [in the gum base] **don't** break down easily.
→ [ ]는 앞의 명사 The chemicals를 수식하는 전치사구이다
→ 문장의 주어가 The chemicals로 복수 명사이므로, 복수형 동사 don't가 쓰였다.

⑬ **Swallowing gum is** usually harmless, but don't *make it a habit*.
→ Swallowing gum은 주어 역할을 하는 동명사구이며, 동명사구는 단수 취급하므로 단수형 동사 is가 쓰였다.
→ 「make A B」는 'A를 B로 만들다'의 의미로, 여기서는 it이 A, a habit이 B에 해당한다.

⑭ [**Swallowing** too much gum at once] can cause digestive problems!
→ [ ]는 주어 역할을 하는 동명사구이다.

본책 • pp. 82-83

3

정답　1 ②　2 ②　3 ④　4 블루베리를 너무 좋아해서 치아가 파랗게 되었기 때문에

문제 해설

1　블루투스의 이름의 유래에 관한 글이므로, 제목으로는 ② '블루투스가 어떻게 그 이름을 얻었는가'가 가장 알맞다.
① 기기를 연결하는 방법　　　　　③ 블루투스: 유용한 기술
④ 유명한 왕들의 재미있는 별명　　⑤ 역사상 가장 위대한 왕은 누구인가?

2 '그 뒤에는 흥미로운 이야기가 있다'는 내용의 주어진 문장은, 이름이 어디서 왔는지 질문을 제기하는 문장 ④와 그에 대한 이야기를 시작하는 문장 ⑤ 사이인 ②의 위치가 가장 알맞다.

3 문장 ⑪에 언급되어 있다.

4 문장 ⑧-⑨에 언급되어 있다.

본문 해석

블루투스는 기기를 연결하는 무선 기술이다. 이것은 스마트폰, 스피커, 그리고 이어폰과 같은 것들에 의해 이용된다! 그런데 블루투스는 왜 '블루투스'라 불릴까? 그 이름은 어디서 왔을까? 그 뒤에는 흥미로운 이야기가 있다.

10세기에 한 왕이 있었다. 그의 이름은 Harald Gormsson이었다. 그는 덴마크와 노르웨이를 통합한 것으로 유명했다. 그는 블루베리를 너무 좋아해서 치아가 파랗게 되었다! 그래서 사람들은 그를 '블루투스'라고 불렀다.

블루투스의 기술자들이 Harald 왕의 별명을 따서 그것을 이름 지었다. 그가 서로 다른 땅을 통합한 것처럼 그것은 서로 다른 기기를 연결했다.

구문 해설

① Bluetooth is a wireless technology **to connect** devices.
➥ to connect는 명사구 a wireless technology를 수식하는 형용사적 용법의 to부정사이다.

② This is used by things **like** smartphones, speakers, and earphones!
➥ like는 '~ 같은'의 의미인 전치사로 쓰였으며, 뒤에 예시에 해당하는 내용이 온다.

⑦ He was famous for **unifying** Denmark and Norway.
➥ unifying은 전치사 for의 목적어 역할을 하는 동명사이다.

⑧ He loved blueberries **so much that** his teeth *became blue*!
➥ 「so+부사[형용사]+that ~」은 '너무 ~해서 …하다'의 의미이다.
➥ 「become+형용사」는 '~해지다'의 의미이다.

⑨ So people **called him** "Bluetooth."
➥ 「call A B」는 'A를 B라고 부르다'의 의미이다.

⑩ The engineers of Bluetooth **named** it **after** King Harald's nickname.

　➡ 「name A after B」는 'B의 이름을 따서 A를 이름 짓다'의 의미이다.

⑪ It connected different devices **like** he unified different lands.

　➡ like는 '~처럼'의 의미인 접속사로 쓰여 뒤에 「주어(he)+동사(unified)」의 절이 이어졌다.

정답 **1** stamp **2** stomach **3** connect **4** push **5** sign **6** engineer **7** ⓑ **8** ⓐ
9 ⓒ **10** ① **11** ③ **12** is famous for **13** According to **14** name, after
15 He loved blueberries so much that his teeth became blue!
16 some parts of it break down in your stomach
17 They tell you to watch out for Santa.

문제
해설

1 stamp: 우표

2 stomach: 위, 복부

3 connect: 연결하다

4 push: 밀다, 밀어내다

5 sign: 표지판

6 engineer: 엔지니어, 기술자

7 lucky(운이 좋은): ⓑ 좋은 운을 가진

8 swallow(삼키다): ⓐ 음식을 입에서 위로 가게 하다

9 unify(통합하다): ⓒ 두 가지 이상의 것을 합쳐 하나로 만들다

10 너는 왜 고향을 떠나기를 원하니?
① 머무르다   ② 받다   ③ 보내다   ④ 방문하다   ⑤ 선택하다

11 그 거미는 무서워 보이지만, 그것은 무해하다.
① 매우 좋아하는   ② 좋은   ③ 해가 되는   ④ 유명한   ⑤ 무선의

12 be famous for: ~로 유명하다

13 according to: ~에 따르면

14 name after: ~의 이름을 따서 명명하다

15 '너무 ~해서 …하다'의 의미로 「so+부사+that ~」을 쓴다. '~해지다'라는 의미는 「become+형용사」로 쓴다.

16 명사구 some parts를 수식하는 전치사구 of it을 쓴다. '분해하다'라는 의미는 break down을 쓴다.

17 '~에게 …하라고 말하다'라는 의미로 「tell+목적어+to-v」를 쓴다. '~에 대해 주의하다'라는 의미는 watch out for로 쓴다.

문법

초등 Grammar Inside

많은 양의 문제를 통해
초등 영문법 기초 다지기

1 | 2 | 3 | 4 | 5 | 6

🔗 Grammar Inside

GRAMMAR BEAN

문법을 처음 시작하는
초급 학습자를 위한 문법서

1 | 2 | 3 | 4

GRAMMAR BUDDY

초등학생을 위한 문법 입문서

1 | 2 | 3

🔗 Reading Buddy | Listening Buddy

듣기

능률 초등영어 듣기모의고사 10회

초등부터 중등까지!
영어 듣기평가 실전 대비서

4-1 | 4-2 | 5-1 | 5-2 | 6-1 | 6-2

초등영어 LISTENING TUTOR

주제별 표현 학습을 바탕으로
듣기 기초를 다지는 초등 리스닝 기본서

Beginner 1 | Beginner 2 | Beginner 3 |
Intermediate 1 | Intermediate 2 |
Intermediate 3

LISTENING BUDDY

초등학생을 위한 리스닝 입문서

1 | 2 | 3

🔗 Reading Buddy | Grammar Buddy

예비중 · 중등

능률 중학영어

문법, 독해, 쓰기, 말하기를
함께 배우는 중학 영어 종합서

예비중 | 중1 | 중2 | 중3

문제로 마스터하는 중학영문법

많은 문제로 확실히 끝내는 중학 영문법

Level 1 | Level 2 | Level 3

🔗 문제로 마스터하는 고등 영문법

GRAMMAR Inside

많은 양의 문제로 체계적으로
학습하는 중학 영문법

Starter | Level 1 | Level 2 | Level 3

JUNIOR READING EXPERT

앞서가는 중학생들을 위한 원서형 독해 교재

Level 1 | Level 2 | Level 3 | Level 4

능률 중학영어 듣기 모의고사 22회

전국 16개 시·도 교육청 주관
영어듣기평가 실전대비서

Level 1 | Level 2 | Level 3

NE능률 영어교육연구소

NE능률 영어교육연구소는 전문성과 탁월성을 기반으로
영어 교육 트렌드를 선도합니다.

조 은 영 선임연구원　　**권 영 주** 선임연구원
김 영 아 연구원　　　　**최 　 리** 연구원

펴 낸 날	2025년 1월 5일 (초판 1쇄)　2025년 9월 15일 (제4쇄)
펴 낸 이	주민홍
펴 낸 곳	(주)NE능률
지 은 이	NE능률 영어교육연구소
개 발 책 임	김지현
개 　 발	조은영, 권영주, 김영아, 최리
영 문 교 열	Patrick Ferraro, Julie Tofflemire, Keeran Murphy
디 자 인 책 임	오영숙
디 자 인	안훈정, 오솔길, 민유화
제 작 책 임	한성일
등 록 번 호	제1-68호
I S B N	979-11-253-4853-5

＊이 책의 저작권은 (주)NE능률에 있습니다.
＊본 교재의 독창적인 내용에 대한 일체의 무단 전재 모방은 법률로 금지되어 있습니다.

대 표 전 화	02 2014 7114
홈 페 이 지	www.neungyule.com
주 　 소	서울시 마포구 월드컵북로 396(상암동) 누리꿈스퀘어 비즈니스타워 10층